Request Sequences

Studies in Discourse and Grammar

Studies in Discourse and Grammar is a monograph series providing a forum for research on grammar as it emerges from and is accounted for by discourse contexts. The assumption underlying the series is that corpora reflecting language as it is actually used are necessary, not only for the verification of grammatical analyses, but also for understanding how the regularities we think of as grammar emerge from communicative needs.

Research in discourse and grammar draws upon both spoken and written corpora, and it is typically, though not necessarily, quantitative. Monographs in the series propose explanations for grammatical regularities in terms of recurrent discourse patterns, which reflect communicative needs, both informational and socio-cultural.

Editors

Sandra A. Thompson
University of California at Santa Barbara
Department of Linguistics
Santa Barbara, CA 93106
USA

Paul J. Hopper
Carnegie Mellon University
Department of English
Pittsburgh, PA 15213
USA

Volume 19

Request Sequences: The intersection of grammar, interaction and social context
by Carmen Taleghani-Nikazm

Request Sequences

The intersection of grammar,
interaction and social context

Carmen Taleghani-Nikazm

University of Kansas

John Benjamins Publishing Company

Amsterdam/Philadelphia

™ The paper used in this publication meets the minimum requirements
of American National Standard for Information Sciences – Permanence
of Paper for Printed Library Materials, ANSI z39.48-1984.

Library of Congress Cataloging-in-Publication Data

Taleghani-Nikazm, Carmen
    Request Sequences : the intersection of grammar, interaction and social
       context / Carmen Taleghani-Nikazm.
       p. cm. (Studies in Discourse and Grammar, ISSN 0928–8929 ; v. 19)
    Includes bibliographical references and indexes.
       1. Sociolinguistics. 2. Conversational analysis. 3. Social interaction.
    I. Title. II. Series.

    P40.T2574 2006
306.44--dc22   2006040656
ISBN 90 272 2629 6 (Hb; alk. paper)

John Benjamins Publishing Co. · P.O. Box 36224 · 1020 ME Amsterdam · The Netherlands
John Benjamins North America · P.O. Box 27519 · Philadelphia PA 19118-0519 · USA

For Kamel and Nina

Table of contents

Acknowledgements

This book would have not been possible without the support and encouragement of many teachers, colleagues, and friends over the years. I first wish to express my sincerest thanks to Maria Egbert and Jürgen Streeck for introducing me to conversation analysis, and for having been constant sources of invaluable advice and continual support through my graduate career at the University of Texas at Austin and beyond. I also wish to express my gratitude to Mark Louden for his guidance and encouragement throughout my graduate studies. All three of them have contributed immensely to my career as a researcher of language use and as a teacher; all three of them have likewise served for me as examples of caring human beings. I also would like to extend my thanks to Emanuel Schegloff, John Heritage, Gene Lerner, and the participants of the 2002 Conversation Analysis Advanced Study Institute at UCLA for their helpful comments and suggestions on early ideas for this book. I am especially grateful to Emanuel Schegloff for kindly providing me with invaluable feedback on preliminary stages of this project.

I wish to express my deep indebtedness to Andrea Golato and Peter Golato, my close friends and colleagues, who so generously made time to carefully read various versions of this manuscript. Their constructive criticism and insightful feedback at various stages of this project contributed immensely to fine tuning my analyses. My thanks also go to Maria Egbert for her insightful comments and suggestions on various parts of this manuscript.

I would like to express my deepest gratitude to relatives, friends and graduate students in the United States and Germany for their help and support during the data collection phase of this work. This book would not have been possible without their generosity and kind participation.

A part of chapter 5 has been published in *Research on Language and Social Interaction*, Vol. 38, No. 2 (Lawrence Erlbaum, 2005). I am grateful to the anonymous reviewers for their insightful and stimulating commentaries.

This project was supported by funds from the University of Kansas and the Fulbright Scholar Program. I am thankful for their support of various parts of this project.

Finally, my special thanks goes to my husband Kamel Nikazm for his love and unconditional support. Without his understanding, encouragement, and enthusiasm I could not have completed this manuscript. I am also tremendously grateful to our daughter Nina for her patience and good humor during some stressful times, as the completion of this project would have been immeasurably more difficult without her cooperation. It is to both of them that I gratefully dedicate this book.

CHAPTER 1

Preliminaries

1.1. Introduction

The present book involves a descriptive micro-analysis of the interplay between the linguistic realization of utterances (grammar) and the type of actions they carry out (interaction) in their broader sequential and contextual conversational environment. The book accomplishes this through systematic analyses of one particular social action, that of requests in everyday German discourse. Request in everyday conversation refers here to a type of social action in which the interactional goal of the first speaker is to get his or her co-participant to perform an action (i.e., transferring something of value, for example an object, service or information) that is for the benefit of the first speaker or a third party. The requested action may be performed at the time of speaking or at some later point (Gohl 2000; Scott 1987; Schegloff in press).

Using conversation analytic methodology, the present study explores the grammatical and syntactical structure of the request-turn and its response and of the conversational exchanges before, within, and after the request base sequence, and the placement of the request sequence within the larger social interaction. Through an empirical analysis of individual cases of request sequences in German, the present book describes in detail: (a) how speakers deploy grammar and syntax as resources to construct turns at talk and accomplish the social action of request; (b) how speakers use grammatical and syntactical form of the language to coordinate the production of the social action of requests; (c) how speakers use grammar and syntax as interactional resources to manage affiliative and remedial work when performing a request, and (d) how the request activity context impacts the grammatical construction of speakers' utterances. Additionally, the book demonstrates that not only the grammatical construction of turns, but also their placement within the talk is oriented to the sequential context of the interaction. Overall, this book is part of a larger research program (Fox 1996; Ochs, Schegloff, and Thompson 1996; Selting and Couper-Kuhlen 2001) which involves the investigation of grammatical regularities and their functions in human social interaction. In its broadest sense, the present study seeks to further our understanding of human conduct and of the social activities and organization which arise from it.

1.2.   The study of requests in their sequential context

The social action of requesting has received a great deal of attention in the fields of linguistics and applied linguistics. The majority of studies in these fields have investigated the activity of requesting with the goal of exploring and contrasting politeness strategies in various cultures.[1] Overall, the rationale for selecting the speech act of request in these studies is that its modes of performance carry heavy social implications and seem to be ruled by universal principles of cooperation and politeness; thus, in a requestive situation, researchers might find more politeness in the interactants' language. Studies indicate that while there are universal pragmatic principles underlying speech act performance in all the languages examined, the way in which these principles are applied and the context of their application can vary cross-culturally.[2] It should be pointed out, however, that these studies conducted their cross-cultural study within the conceptual framework of speech act theory, analyzing compositional features of isolated and decontextualized sentences which were elicited through role plays and/or discourse completion tasks. As a result, their findings are based solely upon the examination of isolated request sentences, and thus tend not to reflect the speech situation as a whole. Some researchers, for example House and Kasper (1981), in fact address this methodological shortcoming, and note that elicited data does not provide a fully "authentic" picture of the spontaneous use of spoken language and that therefore, further investigations including the entire discourse context are warranted. The present study will represent a partial answer to House and Kasper's (1981) call for further research on the linguistic and interactional features of requests. Using Conversation Analysis (CA), an empirical methodology that studies the organization of naturally occurring conversations which have been captured on either video-tape or audio-tape, this study examines the basic mechanisms of request sequences within the context of everyday German conversations, using both the speakers' and the recipients' verbal behaviors in recorded talk-in-interactions.

With its focus on "language in use", CA examines the discourse which members of a society produce for each other within the activities that constitute their context. CA does not make use of interviews, native intuitions and/or questionnaires; from a CA perspective, such introspective/intuitive accounts of conversational practices are unreliable because they are generally thought to reflect *naïve* intuitions concerning what participants should say, rather than what they actually *do* say. As Atkinson and Heritage (1984: 3) note on the use of experimentally produced data:

> while certain of the experimenter's data may or may not be artifacts of the more general experimental situation in which the data were produced such influences (if any) can be determined only by systematic comparison with a large corpus of

naturally occurring data. The most economical procedure, therefore, has been to work on naturally occurring materials from the outset. Naturally occurring interaction presents an immense range of circumstances – effectively amounting to a "natural laboratory" – for the pursuit of hunches and the investigation of the limits of particular formulations by systematic comparison.

Experimentally produced data such as elicited role plays or written version of talk are, therefore, unable to capture pragmatic dimensions of the conversational practices they are eliciting. CA is thus the most tenable methodology for the analysis of spontaneous conversation, since it aims to reveal the interactional orientations of the speakers in context through closely analyzing the details of the conversation (Seedhouse 1998: 101). With respect to spontaneous conversation, Heritage (1984a: 241) offers the following three fundamental assumptions that form the underlying beliefs of conversation analysis: "(1) interaction is structurally organized; (2) contributions to interaction are contextually oriented; and (3) these two properties inhere in the details of interaction so that no order of detail can be dismissed, *a priori,* as disorderly, accidental or irrelevant."

The first and most basic underlying assumption is that social action and interaction are inherently orderly. According to this basic assumption, social actors are assumed to posses a knowledge of the orderliness or regularities of the interaction; this influences their conduct as well as their understanding of their co-participant's action. Conversation analytical studies thus seek to uncover how participants orient to these regularities and organizational patterns of social actions. The second fundamental assumption holds that speakers' contributions to interaction are tightly connected to the local context in which utterances are produced. Heritage (1984a) notes that a speaker's contribution is both "context-shaped" and "context-renewing" (242). That is, a speaker's turn at talk is "context-shaped" in that it can only be adequately interpreted by its co-participants by reference to the context within which it was produced. A speaker's turn is also "context-renewing" since any given utterance forms the immediate context for the next action and the framework within which the action will be understood. Put differently, each turn at talk is contextual, in that each turn is shaped by the context of prior talk and that each turn establishes a context to which the next turn will be oriented. The third fundamental assumption holds that all discovered details in social interaction, verbal or non-verbal, deserve scrutiny since they provide researchers with an understanding of the underlying structure of interaction. With its focus on real-time interactional language use, CA has been used in sociolinguistics, anthropology, and communication studies, and is well suited for any researcher who examines language in its actual use.

The present study differs from previous work on the social action of request in that it examines the mechanisms of sequential organization of request in the contextual environment of German conversation. In particular, this study's close analysis of the sequential organization of requests in German will uncover the ways in which participants construct and accomplish the social action of requesting in real time. In addition to the description of the sequential organization of requests, the present study demonstrates how participants orient to the context of their action, i.e. making a request. In this sense, the present study serves as a description of some language-general features (i.e., not specific to German) of the sequential organization of requests in real-time interactional language use.

1.3.   Preference organization and its relevance to social solidarity

One key concept central to the analysis of sequential organization of requests is "preference organization" (Atkinson and Heritage 1984; Heritage 1985; Hutchby and Wooffitt 1999; Levinson 1983; Schegloff in press). The underlying idea is that turns at talk are sequentially ordered; that is, they are sequentially linked to one another in the sense that, as discussed above, each turn at talk is shaped by the context of prior talk and that each turn establishes a context to which the next turn will be oriented. Social activities such as requests, offers, invitations, etc., occur in pairs (minimally) where one speaker produces the first part (e.g., an offer) and the second speaker the second part (e.g., an acceptance or a rejection). This basic unit of sequences, i.e., the first pair part and the second pair part is called "adjacency pairs" (Schegloff and Sacks 1973; Schegloff in press). An important feature of the relationship between the first and second pair part is the notion of preference structure. According to this notion, there is a set of possible responses to a first part; however, elements of this set are frequently not treated by interactants as equivalent choices, in that one second part will be preferred over the others. For example, in English, a preferred response to an offer is an acceptance, while a dispreferred response is a rejection (Davidson 1984; Schegloff in press). Generally, preferred responses or activities are produced immediately and briefly. In contrast, dispreferred responses or activities exhibit a more elaborate turn structure: they are frequently produced with some sort of hesitation, hedges (e.g., "uhm", "well"), mitigation, and accounts (Davidson 1984; Heritage 1984a; Levinson 1983; Pomerantz 1984; Schegloff in press). It should be noted that the concept of preference does not refer to speakers' psychological motives and intentions, but rather to the design of turns associated with preferred or dispreferred activities (Heritage 1984a).

Preference organization does not exclusively apply to the design of response turns or second parts: the first pair parts of certain social activities have also been found to be sequentially preferred practices. For example, it has been suggested that requests and offers are sequentially related and that offers are preferred activities over requests (Heritage 1984a; Lerner 1996a; Levinson 1983; Sacks 1996; Schegloff 1990, 1995). Similar to dispreferred response activities, dispreferred first actions may exhibit structural features of the turn design associated with dispreferred action formats, such as delays, accounts and mitigations.

The aforementioned systematic design of preferred and dispreferred turns is fundamentally tied to the actions themselves by which participants can interpret a turn (Davidson 1984; Heritage 1984a). Davidson (1984) notes that speakers have resources available to them which they may employ as devices to project and/or inhibit the production of dispreferred first parts. For example, delays are devices that may give the co-participants the opportunity to project the potentially "dispreferred" rejections of invitations, thus affording the inviter an opportunity to reformulate his or her invitation to elicit acceptance (Davidson 1984).

Another important procedure which enables co-participants to collaborate to forward preferred actions and avoid dispreferred ones is the pre-sequence (Heritage 1984a; Lerner 1996a; Levinson 1983; Schegloff 1990, 1995). Pre-sequences are inserted before the first pair part of the adjacency pair and are considered to be preliminary to the first pair part (Schegloff 1980). Such expansions are for example pre-invitations, e.g., "what are you doing this evening?", or pre-requests, e.g., "can you do me a favor?". These "pre"'s all engender their own sequences; they are themselves first pair parts and make a response relevant as a next action. Many pre-sequences are type-specific pre-sequences, i.e. they project a particular sequence type such as an invitation, announcement, etc. More to the point, pre-sequences explore the likelihood that the actions projected will not be responded to in a dispreferred way. For example, an utterance such as "what are you doing tonight?" can easily be interpreted by the recipient as a pre-invitation or pre-request. The recipient's response to the first pair part of a pre-invitation may influence the outcome of the next action performed by the producer of the pre-invitation, and it might lead to an actual invitation, or to other talk if the recipient has prior engagements.

According to Goodwin and Heritage (1990), pre-sequences provide specific advantages both to their producer, and to their recipients. First, pre-sequences enable parties to abort a projected interaction sequence in which conflict, disagreement, or rejection might emerge. Second, if the projected sequence is not aborted in this way, an affiliative outcome becomes more likely. For example, a pre-sequence that anticipates a request may elicit an offer from the hearer. Seen in this way, pre-sequences are conversational devices through which dispreferred, face-threatening actions and sequences can be systematically avoided in interaction (Heritage 1984a; Lerner 1996a; Levinson 1983; Schegloff in press): by using pre-sequences to forestall possible rejection turns, co-participants minimize the occurrence of such turns and thereby promote social solidarity (Heritage 1984a).

To reiterate, preferred and dispreferred responses are structured in a way to enhance the performance of preferred responses, and to inhibit the performance of dispreferred responses (Davidson 1984; Goodwin and Heritage 1990; Heritage 1984a; Pomerantz 1984, Schegloff in press). The specific design of preferred and dispreferred action types is related to their affiliative and disaffiliative character-istics: the preferred responses to requests, invitations, and offers are affiliative actions and thus supportive of social solidarity, while dispreferred responses are largely disaffiliative and destructive of social solidarity (Goodwin and Heritage 1990; Heritage 1984a). That is, speakers follow patterns of behavior to interact with one another smoothly and to minimize the risk of confrontation. By performing preferred actions and avoiding dispreferred actions, speakers display to each other their cooperativeness and support solidarity (Goodwin and Heritage 1990).

Looking closely at the sequential organization of request, the present study explores how speakers display, through the sequencing of their utterances, their orientation to the preference organization of requests. In particular, the study examines ways in which speakers design their turns when engaged in the dispre-ferred activity of requesting. In particular, the analysis focuses on ways speakers manage affiliative conversational moves when requesting. This is achieved by detailed analyses of the grammatical composition of speakers' utterances in the sequential and contextual environment of making requests, and the type of social actions they achieve.

1.4. The interpenetration of grammar and social interaction

The present research is in line with the growing body of work on the interplay between the organization of grammar and the organization of human conduct, particularly social interaction (e.g., Ford 1993; Ford, Fox and Thompson 2002; Golato 2005; Hayashi 2003; Koshik 2005; Lerner 1991; Ochs et al. 1996; Selting and Couper-Kuhlen 2001). Working within the conversation analytic and interactional linguistic frameworks, these researchers view language as jointly constructed by interactants in socially organized activities. Researchers within these frameworks investigate language *in situ*, that is, they work on recorded data from naturally occurring conversation rather than elicited non-interactional forms of language, and view language as an object through which speakers accom-plish particular social actions through their interactions with one another. One core element of their study has been grammar in its "natural habitat" (Ford, 1993: 1), i.e., in contextualized verbal interaction. In particular, they study grammar and its operation and emergence in talk-in-interaction (rather than in abstract sentences), and as a result propose a different view and understanding of grammar and its relationship to social interaction:

> Grammar is not only a resource for interaction and not only an outcome of interaction, it is part of the essence of interaction itself. Or, to put it another way, grammar is inherently interactional.   (Schegloff et al. 1996: 38)

That is, grammar is understood as a phenomenon which is tightly intertwined with social interaction. Within this tradition, a wide range of studies have documented how grammatical forms are used by speakers as a resource for constructing social actions. Some have focused on turns at talk, their grammatical forms, and co-participant's orientations to their grammatical structure (e.g., Ford 1993; 2001; Ford and Mori 1994; Ford and Thompson 1996; Golato 2005; Koshik 2005; Sacks, Schegloff, and Jefferson 1974; Schegloff 1996), whereas others have concentrated on one particular grammatical component and its interactional function (e.g., Heritage 2002; Lerner 2004; Mori 1999; Raymond 2004; Scheutz 2001; Sorjonen 2002; Turk 2004). In addition to this view that grammar organizes social interaction, researchers have also focused on how grammatical forms are influenced by social actions. These studies have documented how the sequential and activity context shapes grammatical forms by focusing on various social contexts such as complimenting and responding to compliments (Golato 2002a, 2005) question design in institutional and everyday settings (Koshik 2005), reported speech (Couper-Kuhlen 1999; Golato 2000, 2002b, 2002c), and the usage of particles and response tokens (Hayashi 1997; Sorjonen 1996, 2001). Another thematic focus of research on the interpenetration of grammar and social interaction is the view of grammar as "a mode of social interaction" (Schegloff et al. 1996: 38). In this context, studies have focused on the dynamic co-construction of turns at talk and demonstrated how the real-time linguistic construction of an utterance emerges in response to local contingencies over interactional time (Ford and Thompson 1996; Goodwin 1979, 1981, 1996; Hayashi 1999; Lerner 1987, 1991, 1993, 1996a, 1996b, 2002; Schegloff 1979, 1996).

The research on the reflexive relationship between grammar and social interaction has also taken a cross-linguistic direction. Researchers have examined linguistic constructions in naturally occurring talk in a variety of settings in such typologically diverse languages as Japanese (Ford and Mori 1994 on causal conjunctions; Fox, Hayashi, and Jasperson 1996; Hayashi 1994 on repair; Hayashi 1999, Hayashi and Mori 1998, Hayashi, Mori, and Takagi 2002 on collaborative construction), German (Egbert 1996, 1997; Golato 2000, 2002b, 2002c; Günthner 1999a on reported discourse; Golato 2002a, 2005 on complimenting sequences; Gohl 2000; Günthner 1996; Scheutz 2001; Taleghani-Nikazm 2005 on causal clauses; Uhman 2001 on repair), and Finnish (Sorjonen 1996, 2001a, 2001b on response tokens), among others. Building upon research with English interactional data on the interface between grammar and interaction, these researchers demonstrate how, in a given language, the grammatical construction of turns at talk may be influenced by the social interaction, and how the sequential context of the social activity may shape the grammatical composition of the turns. Furthermore, these studies have focused on how this reflexive relationship between grammar and social interaction is molded by the particularities of the language under study.

The present research builds upon the aforementioned body of work, and expands the discussion of grammar and interaction by focusing on one particular social action, namely that of requests in everyday German conversation. As mentioned in the previous section, the social action of requests has been described by conversation analysts as a "dispreferred" practice compared to offers. As such, speakers utilize interactional devices to project the possibility of the occurrence of a request and hence to impede the occurrence of such a dispreferred action. Furthermore, when produced, first parts of requests may exhibit a dispreferred action format. The social action of request was chosen for this investigation since it provides a fruitful site for exploring the ways in which grammar is tightly interwoven with the interactional activities in which people are engaged. The present study makes a contribution to the field in that it documents the grammatical resources speakers use to design their pre-request turns, their responses, and the resulting offer and request turns. The study pays close attention to: (a) how the grammatical and syntactical pre-request and request turn shapes are influenced by the underlying structure of social interaction, i.e., the management of affiliative moves and the maintenance of social solidarity, and (b) how the emergence of a social activity such as request (and its particularities) give rise to the grammatical shape that turns take.

1.5. Overview of the book

Chapter 2 discusses some structural characteristics of the German language, and presents an overview of grammatical regularities prescribed by German grammar references for request formulations. In addition, the chapter offers a description of the data collection procedure and concludes with a description of the subjects used for the present study.

Chapter 3 provides a description of the ways in which utterances accomplish particular actions by virtue of their placement within sequences of actions.

In particular, it focuses on the sequential context in which speakers' turns are analyzed by their recipients as pre-requests, and how this is displayed in the recipients' next turns. Additionally, chapter 3 presents an analysis of how both pre-request turns and their responses are linguistically constructed and how pre-requests and their subsequent talk, i.e., their expansions, occasion the type of requests speakers make.

Chapter 4 continues exploring the relationship between the grammatical construction and interactional function of utterances by focusing on another design feature of request sequences. Specifically, the chapter provides an analysis of request sequences in which speakers provide their co-participants with an explanation or justification for their request. Furthermore, the chapter demonstrates that the composition, syntax, and sequential placement of accounts for request turns may result in the requests having different interactional functions.

Chapter 5 focuses on the connection between the position of particular units in a turn and the turn type. The chapter discusses how speakers initiate their pre-request turn with an idiomatic phrase, thereby signaling the pre-request turn's relationship to prior talk and providing co-participants with resources for project-ability, i.e., allowing co-participants to prefigure (anticipate) aspects of the turn. In other words, the chapter shows how speakers allow their co-participants to prefigure in what direction the turn is going by initially placing idiomatic expression in pre-requests.

Chapter 6 presents the conclusions of the present study by summarizing its findings and offering a discussion of some implications of this type of work. Directions for future research are also indicated in this chapter.

Notes

1. For studies on the linguistic realization of requests in various cultures see: Blum-Kulka and Oshtain 1984; Blum-Kulka 1987 for Hebrew; Blum-Kulka, S., House, J. and Kasper, G. 1989 for American English, Canadian French, Hebrew, Argentinian Spanish, Russian, German, Thai; Brown and Levinson 1987 for English, Tamil and Tzeltal; Eslamirasekh 1993; Moosavie 1986 for Persian; House and Kasper 1981; House 1989 for German; Fukushima 1996 for Japanese; Garcia 1993 for Spanish; Koike 1989, 1994 for Spanish and English; Leech 1983 for English; Márquez Reiter 2000 for Uruguayn Spanish and British English; Pair 1996 for Spanish and Dutch; Sifiano 1993 for Greek; Trosborg 1995 for Danish and English; Van Mulken 1996 for French and Dutch.

2. It should be noted that the majority of the comparative studies on requests and politeness were inspired by Brown and Levinson's negative and positive politeness

theory (1987). The aim of these studies was to improve our understanding of universal politeness phenomena and the ways in which they are realized in different languages and cultures.

CHAPTER 2

Overview of the methodology and corpus

The chapter begins with a summary of previous studies on requests in German. This is followed by a brief overview of the grammatical regularities prescribed by German grammar references for request formulations. The chapter concludes with a description of the corpus and the transcription conventions used in this book.

2.1. Previous studies on requests in German

In everyday conversation, speakers regularly ask their co-participants to perform an action that is for the benefit of themselves or a third party. Overall, the social activity of request has attracted many researchers in the field of sociolinguistics and second language acquisition (Blum-Kulka, S. House, J. and Kasper, G. 1989; Brown and Levinson 1978, 1987; Eslamirasekh 1993; Fukushima 1996; Garcia 1993; House and Kasper 1981; le Pair 1996; Sifiano 1993; Van Mulken 1996). The core motivation for studying requests has been the assumption that the activity is "intrinsically impolite" and carries heavy social implications, and is therefore governed by putative principles of politeness (Blum-Kulka, S. House, J. and Kasper, G. 1989; Brown and Levinson 1978, 1987). Thus, when making a request, speakers will use politeness strategies to minimize the threat that is intrinsically present within them.

As was mentioned in chapter 1, the majority of these studies have explored requests in the context of cross-cultural comparisons of politeness strategies. The focus of these studies has been on examining similarities and differences between politeness strategies employed by speakers of different languages when producing requests. In general, these studies adopted the "Cross-Cultural Speech Act Realization Project", or CCSARP, analytical method, developed by Blum-Kulka et al. (1989) using discourse completion tasks and production questionnaires as the method of data collection.[1] Inspired by Leech's (1983) and Brown and Levinson's (1978, 1987) politeness theories, these researchers examined requests and apologies in a number of languages (English, Canadian French, Hebrew, Argentinian Spanish, Russian, German, and Thai) by focusing on ways in which language is used to perform these two speech acts, together with the social and situational variables that potentially affect their use. Focusing on conversational strategy types such as directness, indirectness, and "internal and external" modifications,[2] these studies of requests have illustrated that the relative importance played by social distance, situational settings, and degree of imposition may differ from culture to culture, and that the availability and use of more direct versus more indirect strategies will be culture-specific. Taken together, results of these studies suggest that indirectness and politeness are not necessary correlates of each other, either universally or within a given culture.

Requests in German have also been studied within the aforementioned context of politeness strategy research (House and Kasper 1981; House 1989). For instance, using elicited role plays as their corpus,[3] House and Kasper (1981) compared politeness strategies employed by speakers of German and English when producing requests in given social situations.[4] In their study, House and Kasper used a directness level schema as an instrument to measure degree of politeness. With reference to this schema, the researchers noted that Germans selected higher levels of directness in requests compared to English speakers and that they employed different strategies from English speakers in order to mitigate request actions. Overall, House and Kasper's analysis suggested that for mitigating requests, English speakers have a preference for using syntactic means, e.g., "well can you *er can you* prescribe anything for the allergy" while German speakers tend to use lexical means such as modality markers, e.g., "ja können Sie mir *dann vielleicht* was gegen die Allergie verschreiben". House and Kasper proposed that their German subjects used modal particles such as *ja* (yes), *mal* (just), *wohl* (well), *einfach* (simply), *dann* (then), and *vielleicht* (maybe) in their request sentences in order to soften the impact of their utterance on its recipient (177–180).

As part of the CCSARP, House (1989) conducted a cross-cultural study of how German native speakers, German learners of English, and British native speakers use English politeness marker "please" and the German politeness marker *bitte* (please) in the context of requests. The motivation for her study came from House and Kasper's 1981 study, in which they observed that German *bitte* (please) was used more frequently and differently than the equivalent English "please". House (1989) noted that the choice of certain request strategies is more closely connected to the use of the markers *bitte* and "please". The analysis of her data suggested two request strategies in which the German marker *bitte* occurred: the most direct request strategy, i.e., the imperative; and the conventionally indirect strategy (for example, "can you/could you….."). Furthermore, in her analysis of how German learners of English produce elicited request utterances, House observed that in particular situations, German learners of English used the English marker "please" more frequently than did English speakers. House attributed this distribution of the usage of "please" to possible pragmatic transfer from the subjects' native language (German).

The above-mentioned studies on requests in German have assuredly enhanced our general understanding of German pragmatics and linguistics. However, like most available studies of requests, the findings of German requests are based upon examinations of the compositional features of isolated request sentences, focusing on the semantics of individual elements in request sentences and the illocutionary force they may carry. In keeping with their methodological frame-work, these researchers only examined the actual requests themselves, which were produced in unnatural situations; these studies did not consider how recipients oriented to the request sentences. As a result, these studies did not examine the entire real-time discourse in which requests are produced, including conversa-tional strategies which may occur before and after a given request sentence. If our goal is to better understand the ways in which interactants employ language as a resource for performing requests within particular social contexts and in real-time interaction, we ought to examine the sequential organization of requests using naturalistically collected conversations. As Schegloff (1988: 61) notes, "utter-ances are in turns, and turns are parts of sequences; sequences and the projects done through them enter constitutively into utterances like the warp in a woven fabric". Therefore, if we are interested in how requests are linguistically structured in various social contexts, we ought to investigate their occurrences and construc-tions in the wider context of social interaction. As Schegloff et al. (1996: 40) have noted, "The meaning of any single grammatical construction is interactionally contingent, built over interactional time in accordance with interactinal actuali-ties. Meaning lies not with the speaker nor the addressee nor the utterance alone as many philosophical arguments have considered, but rather with the interactional past, current and projected next moment". In this view, the meaning of any gram-matical construction is interactionally contingent and built over interactional time. For these reasons, the present study uses audio recorded and video taped spontaneous, naturally occurring conversations for the investigation of request sequences in German.

2.3. Requests in German as prescribed in reference and learner grammar textbooks

The formulation of requests has also been addressed in German reference and learner grammar books. As with the majority of previous investigations, however, descriptions of request-formulations in these grammars are limited to the request sentence itself. According to German grammar texts, a request for a service, an object, or information may be produced as a question containing a modal verb *kannst du* (are you able to) / *könntest du* (could you) / *würdest du* (would you)... and are described as "polite" requests (Eisenberg 1986: 98; Grammatik der deutschen Sprache 1997: 656; Wells 1997: 262). By formulating the request as a question, the speaker orients to the recipient's ability and likelihood to comply with the request in the future (Grammatik der deutschen Sprache 1997:142–143). For example, request-questions with modals such as *Kannst du uns besuchen?* (can you visit us?) or *Kannst du mir den Bohrer geben?* (can you give me the drill?) address the *ability* or *likelihood* of the hearer's performing the requested action (either visiting or giving someone a drill), rather than their *willingness* to perform the requested action. These kinds of requests are frequently accompanied by *Abtö-nungspartikel,* that is, by modal particles which soften the imposition and mitigate the action of request (Duden 1998: 614; Engel 1991: 234; Grammatik der deutschen Sprache 1997:144). So, by way of example, the following sentence containing the modal particles *bitte* and *mal* (just) is described as particularly polite: *Kannst du mir bitte mal das Buch leihen?* (can you possibly lend me the book?). It should be mentioned here that the prescribed compositional features of polite requests were also noted in House and Kasper's 1981 study (see above section).

Another compositional feature suggested by the reference grammars is that request-question utterances including a modal verb may also be produced in the present conditional: for example, *könntest du mir bitte mal das Buch leihen?* (could you possibly lend me the book?). Likewise, it has been suggested that the recipe for a very polite request is to use the subjunctive mood: for instance, *würden Sie bitte etwas leiser sprechen?* (would you please speak a bit quieter?). According to the German reference and learner grammars I consulted, by using modal and auxiliary verbs in the present-subjunctive, speakers are able to weaken the conditionality of the request (Eisenberg 1999; Grammatik der deutschen Sprache 1997; Wells 1997). As I stated earlier, however, these learner and reference grammars of German are limited in the same way as the studies mentioned previously, in that they concentrate only on the compositional features of request sentences and their semantic meanings and *exclude* not only the request response, but also the talk that may occur before or after a given request sentence. Furthermore, the prescribed formulations for "polite" request sentences in grammar references are based solely on written language and on grammarians' intuitions and presumptions of how German request sentences are formulated in spoken discourse.

2.4. Description of the corpus

As mentioned in chapter 1, the present study of the grammatical composition and sequential placement of turns in request sequences will be conducted within the CA framework. The study analyzes social actions and identifies their natural organization through close examination of video-taped or audio-recorded inter-action data, which are transcribed by the researcher using a transcription system developed by Gail Jefferson (1984). In general, research in CA has illustrated that (a) there is a systematicity underlying all conversations, (b) co-participants orient to each other and to the context of their interaction, and (c) no set of detail can be dismissed as "accidental or irrelevant" (Heritage 1984, p. 241). Since CA examines the most routine, everyday, naturally occurring activities in their concrete details, it is essential to work with naturally occurring conversations that have been video-taped or audio-recorded.

The corpus for the present study consists of 21 hours of telephone conversa-tion and 4 hours of face-to-face interaction[5] between relatives and close friends. The situational settings included everyday social gatherings such as dinner-table conversations, coffee-table conversations at private homes and everyday tele-phone conversations, all of which were activities that the participants would normally engage in. The speakers were between 20 and 65 years of age, and were German native speakers.[6] The participants came from different regions in Germany (Hamburg, Bremen, Berlin, Brandenburg, Bamberg, Munich, and Nuremberg) and spoke standard German and regional dialects.[7] A total of 22 speakers were recorded, of which 12 were females. About half of the phone calls were made from the United States by native speakers of German who were living in the United States at the time the phone calls were made.[8] The video-taped face-to-face interactions were all recorded in Germany.[9]

For the present study, I examined only instances of requests for service (action) performed by one of the interactants. The resulting 30 request sequences were those in which the interactional goal of the speaker was to get his or her co-participant to perform an action such as transferring an object, service or information for the benefit of the requester or a third party. The rational for choosing request sequences for the present analysis is that they provide rich examples of ways in which speakers deploy grammar and syntax as resources to construct their turns at talk. Furthermore, considering the main focus of the present study, i.e., the examination of the interpenetration of grammar and social organization, the request sequences exemplified in the present analysis offered a fruitful illustration of how the context of making a dispreferred action of request impacts the grammatical construction of speakers' utterances, and how speakers' turn design organizes the social interaction.

The video-taped and audio-recorded conversations were transcribed according to the conventions developed by Gail Jefferson for research in conversation anal-ysis (see Sacks et al. 1974: 731–734; Jefferson 1984a: ix-xvi). In the transcripts, the top line presents the original German talk. The word-by-word gloss, including grammatical descriptions, is provided in the second line (see the Appendix for abbreviations used for the grammatical descriptions). The English translation is provided in italics in the third line of the turn. Participants' gaze, gesture, and other bodily behavior were only included in the transcript when relevant to the analysis. Since CA transcription convention uses capitalization to mark loudness in conversation, conversation analysts working with the German language usually refrain from capitalizing German nouns (see, for example, Golato 2005).

Notes

1. See Golato 2003 and 2005 for a detailed discussion of various studies that address the inadequacy of intuition in research on language use.

2. "Internal" modifications refer to devices within the same "head act", whereas "external" modifications refer to devices localized not within the same "head act" but within its immediate context (201).

3. House and Kasper's (1981) corpus consisted of 24 situations in which the role relationship between the interlocuters (i.e., authority or lack of authority) and social distance (i.e., formality and informality) varied.

4. After viewing their collected data, House and Kasper (1981) developed a schema of 8 levels of directness, with level 1 being the most indirect and level 8 the most direct. For example, they categorized "mild hints" as the most indirect of requests. In their study, mild hints refer to utterances that do not explicitly express their illocutionary force; therefore, the recipient of such an utterance (who is actually the analyst(s), considering the data collection method) must discover what the utterance (locution) implies.

5. One shortcoming of the data is the limited scope of the corpus in terms of the video-taped face-to-face interactions.

6. Naturally, interactants were not informed about the exact nature of the research so that this knowledge would not influence their interaction. They were told that the data collection was for a research project on everyday spoken language. Pseudonyms are used in the transcripts and analyses in order to maintain the participants' anonymity.

7. The speakers from Bamberg and Nuremberg spoken mainly the regional Franconian dialect.

8. The speakers in these phone conversations were graduate students from German universities who were on an exchange program in a German graduate program at an American university. These native speakers of German had resided in the United States for two months and two years at the time of recording. During their

graduate studies, they were in close contact with other German native speakers in their department and on campus. When examining their recorded conversation, I did not observe any systematic influence of their stay in the United States upon their interactions, other than their usage of certain specific English vocabulary; these minor influences may be attributed to their limited stays in the United States and their frequent interaction with other native speakers.

9. For practical reasons, only gatherings around a dinner table or coffee table were videotaped.

Pre-request and request sequences: Their design, interactional relationship and sequential placement

3.1. Introduction

The purpose of this chapter is twofold: First, it provides a description of ways in which utterances accomplish particular actions by virtue of their placement within sequences of actions. Specifically, it focuses on the sequential context in which speakers' turns are analyzed by their recipients as pre-requests and how this is displayed in the recipients' relevant next turns. Second, it presents an analysis of how both pre-request turns and their responses are linguistically constructed. The last part of this chapter explores the talk that occurs after a pre-request. In particular, it investigates how pre-requests and their subsequent talk, i.e., their expansions, occasion the type of requests speakers make.

3.2. Pre-request sequences

Chapter one offered a review of studies on preference organization in talk-in-interaction in general, and on pre-requests in particular. It has been suggested that both in American English and German conversations, the social activities of offers and requests are sequentially related and that requests are dispreferred practices compared to offers (Lerner 1996a; Levinson 1983; Heritage 1984a; Sacks 1995; Schegloff 1990; Schegloff in press; for American English; Taleghani-Nikazm 2002 for German). This preference for offers over requests can be found in the occurrence of pre-request sequences. Overall, pre-requests can be understood as interactional devices which speakers utilize to project the possibility of the occurrence of a request. Thus pre-requests provide a way to impede such a dispreferred action by eliciting an offer and consequently making a request unnecessary. However, a speaker's turn does not become recognizable as a pre-request until its recipient demonstrably orients to it as an utterance that projects a request sequence. Furthermore, as the following section will show, it is not only the linguistic composition of a turn but also its sequential placements that make a turn recognizable as a pre-request. Golato (2005), for example, notes that German speakers may utilize food assessments as a pre-request to elicit an offer rather than to request more food.[1] This chapter analyzes three types of pre-requests in German everyday conversations. Specifically, the following section demonstrates how (1) a question; (2) an account, and (3) expressing one's likes/dislikes when uttered in a particular sequential context may be heard by its recipient as a pre-request.

3.2.1 Pre-requests in the form of an inquiry

Pre-requests may be composed as a question that inquires about the availability of the object or service to be requested. The first data segment exemplifies such a case. This is a phone conversation between two sisters, Dora and Carla. Dora, who is currently on an exchange program at an American university, will visit her family in the coming winter.

(1) Dora/Carla (Schlittschuh)

```
01      Dora  :   he. he. o::h gott skifahren wäre  was   me   machen
                  he. he. o::h god  skiing         would what we   make
                  he. He. o::h god  skiing         would be something we

02      Dora  :   [können.
                  [could.
                  [could do.
                  [
03 ->   Carla :   [.hhh horch  mal ä:h he:: .hh genau    da    kann ich   dich
                  [.hhh listen MP u:h he:: .hh exactly there can  i     you
                  [.hhh listen u:h     he:: .hh exactly now   i can

04 ->   Carla :   mal  gleich anbaggern brauchst du   ä:hm, im
                  MP   now    bug       need     you  u:hm, in
                  bug you uh:m, do you    need your skates

05 ->   Carla :   winter  semester   wenn du  wieder nüberfliegst   deine
                  winter  semester when you   again  PRX+fly        your
                  in the winter semester when you fly over

06 ->   Carla :   schlittschuh?
                  ice-skates?
                  again?

07              (0.8)

08 ->   Dora  :   ä:hm, pfr: .hh kaum    ä:h ne. .hh ä:-ä: [in law-l-
                  u:hm, pfr: .hh hardly u:h no. .hh u:-u: [in law-l-
                  u:hm, pfr: .hh hardly u:h no. .hh u:-u: [in law-l-
                                                          [
09 ->   Carla :                                          [gut.
                                                          [good.
                                                          [good.
```

```
10 ->   Dora :   lawrence da    gib's  keine  schlittschubahn       also
                 lawrence there give'it no     ice-skating rink      so
                 Lawrence there aren't any     ice-skating rinks so

11      Carla :  gut  wunderbar weil      dann nehm ich die mit   [( )
                 good wonderful because    then take i   them with [( )
                 good wonderful because    then i'll take them     [( )
                                                                   [
12      Dora :                                                     [ne
                                                                   [no
                                                                   [no

13      Dora : kannst   ( )  kannsch-kannst    mit nehmen kannste mal
                can+you  ( )  can+you-can+you  with take   can+you MP
                you can  ( )  you can-you can take them  you can

14      Dora : schleifen lassen wennst wi(h)llst   he hehehe
                sharpen    let     if+you wa(h)nt+you he hehehe
                have  them sharpened if you wa(h)nt   he hehehe

15      Dora : he .hhh [he
                he .hhh [he
                he .hhh [he
                        [
16      Carla:         [ja genau,    zum beispiel ne    ich überlege
                       [yes exactly, for example  right I    think
                       [yea right,   for example  right I've been

17      Carla: weil      i weiss ned selbe  wo     diese dinge  sind
                because   i know not self   where  these things are
                thinking  because I don't know myself where they are
```

After some talk about their plans for Christmas, Carla asks her sister whether she needs her ice-skates in the winter semester when she comes to visit (lines 3–6). Carla's pre-request can be understood as doing some prefatory work to a projected request sequence. Her pre-request turn is designed as a question which occasions a sequence of question-answer. The response to the question may influence the outcome of the projected request sequence. One purpose which pre-sequences generally serve is to explore the likelihood that the projected action will not receive a dispreferred response (Heritage 1984a; Levinson 1983; Schegloff 1980, 1990, 1995). In other words, by designing her pre-request as a question, Carla explores whether her request can be granted or not.

In line 8, Dora replies to Carla's pre-request with *kaum u:h ne.* 'hardly e:h no'. Schegloff suggests three types of responses that are relevant after a pre-request in American English: (1) a "go-ahead" which forwards the projected request sequence; (2) a response which blocks the occurrence of the projected request sequence, and (3) a "pre-emptive response" in which the recipient of the pre-request offers what he or she thinks would be requested (Schegloff 1990; 1995). Dora's "go-ahead" reply type displays the likelihood that the projected request will be responded to in a preferred way, namely that it will be granted. Dora, then, continues her turn with an explanation of why she wouldn't need her ice-skates (line 10). By expressing that she did not need her ice-skates and providing a reason for not needing them, Dora basically gives her sister the "green light" to make her projected request. Carla, however, does not articulate a request; after a few positive assessments (lines 9 and 11) she mentions that she will then take her sister's ice-skates (line 11). Let us take a closer look at Carla's turn composition: note that after a couple of assessments, Carla continues her turn with the subordinating conjunction *weil* 'because' which is characterized as marking causal relations between two utterances[2] (Gohl 2000). By adding a *weil*-clause to her turn, Carla expresses the reason for her action, namely taking her sister's ice-skates. Note also that the causal connector (Ford 1993) *weil* does not follow with an account. Instead, Carla continues her turn with a *dann*-clause (*then*-clause), *dann nehm ich die mit*, which seems to be one of the components of a "compound turn-constructional unit" (Lerner 1991). Lerner describes compound turn-constructional units as turn compound formats that are constructed by a preliminary component and a final component such as in *if X-then Y*. Therefore, Carla's *dann*-clause may be recognized as the "final component" of *if X-then Y* turn format (which in German would be *wenn X-dann Y*). Note, however, that the "preliminary component" (i.e., the *wenn X*) of the compound turn-constructional unit is not articulated. Thus, Carla's turn seems to be a case of "context ellipsis" (Selting 1997). Selting notes that speakers may contract or reduce parts of their utterances in spoken discourse, that their composition or form depends on the given context, and that speakers formulate them in such a way that their co-participant recognizes and interprets the syntactical construction from the sequential context (p. 123).[3] Considering Carla's *dann*-clause content (line 11), we may assume that the phrase *wenn du sie nicht brauchst* 'if you don't need them' is its "preliminary component". Following Carla's turn, Dora suggests that her sister can take the ice-skates (lines 12 and 13). Note that Dora initiates her turn with a negation *ne* (no) which may be addressing Carla's unarticulated or "ellipted" *wenn*-clause. In doing so, Dora displays her understanding of Carla's *dann*-clause as part of a *wenn X-dann Y* construction. Overall, it is evident from Dora's response that she orients to Carla's initial inquiry as a pre-request by first responding with a "go-ahead" type of answer, and then offering the requested object.

It has been argued that "face work" and preference organization are closely related and that speakers use conversational strategies to maintain social solidarity (Levinson 1983; Heritage 1984a). The above example illustrates how an utterance in the linguistic form of a question accomplishes the action of a pre-request. By performing this affiliative conversational strategy, speakers explore the likelihood of receiving a preferred response (i.e., of their request being granted) and thereby enhance social solidarity.

3.2.2   Pre-requests in the form of accounts

Another turn format that pre-requests take is that of accounts. In general, "accounts" in American English and German conversations have been described as actions through which speakers provide descriptions and explanations for their social activities (Gohl 2000; Heritage 1984a; Heritage 1988; Levinson 1983). Normally, accounts occur after the action for which they provide an explanation (Goffman 1971; Gohl 2000; Heritage 1988). The examination of German request sequences suggests that accounts produced in particular interactional environments may be heard by their recipient as pre-requests. In other words, speakers' explanations for their actions or non-actions may be understood by their co-participants as projecting a request sequence, thus making one of the pre-request reply types the conditionally relevant next step. The following excerpt represents an interactional environment in which a pre-request in the form of an account elicits an offer and thereby impedes the production of a projected request. This is a telephone conversation between two colleagues/friends, Martin and Julia, who are members of the same volleyball team. This is the context in which the pre-request occurs: Martin and Julia's volleyball team has a game scheduled for the upcoming Saturday in a different city than where they live. At some point in the conversation (not included in the segment) they start talking about two issues: (a) when to leave for the game (on Friday or on Saturday) and (b) how to get there (asking for a ride from a friend or taking their own car). One concern that comes up during the talk is that if they leave on Friday, they have to camp with the other members. This would mean sleeping in a tent – an idea about which neither of them are very enthusiastic, considering the weather. This would then rule out Friday. Following that conversation, Martin suggests driving together (line 1).

(2)   Martin/Julia (Auto)

```
01    Martin : oder, dann  (  ) wi-wir fahren zusammen.
               or,   then  (  ) w-we   drive  together.
               or,   then  (  ) w-we   drive  together.

02             (1.2)

03    Julia  : also        mir   wirds   schon lieber.
               actually to me    will    MP    rather.
               actually i        would         rather.
```

```
04              (0.5)

05     Martin : ich hab  auch gedacht also     mir ists lieber wenn man
                i    have also thought actually to me is rather if    one
                i    also thought i'd rather have it when you can

06     Martin : freitag einbisschen mal  (0.5) sich  entspannen kann
                friday a little bit MP    (0.5) RXP   relax      can
                first relax a little bit  (0.5) on friday

07     Martin : erstmal
                first+MP
                first+MP

08              (1.2)

09 ->  Julia  : .hhh aber- (0.5)  aber ich >würde  auch   nicht  so
                .hhh but-  (0.5)  but  I   >would  also   not    so
                .hhh but-  (0.5)  but  I   >would  rather not<

10 ->  Julia  : gern< mit  meinem auto  fahren.
                like< with my     car   drive.
                take my car.

11              (0.2)

12 ->  Martin : nicht so gern,?
                not   so like,?
                rather not,?

13 ->  Julia: ne:,  der verliert öl,
              no:,  it loses     oil,
              no:,  it leaks     oil,

14              (.)

15 ->  Martin : ach so    naja wir können ja  mit  meinem auto fahren.
                oh  so    well we  could  MP  with my     car  drive
                oh  i see well we  could  take   my     car

16 ->  Julia:  °und das ist° zum beispiel sehr gut
               °and that is° for example  very good
               °and that's°  for example  very good
```

In line 1, Martin suggests driving together with Julia to the city where the volley-ball game is going to take place. Julia, in turn, agrees with Martin's suggestion (line 3). In lines 5 and 6, Martin provides an account for his offer, namely the benefit of staying home on Friday to relax. After having agreed to leave on Saturday, the next item to be discussed is how to get there; in other words, whose car they should take. At this point in the talk, Julia expresses her wish that they not take her car (lines 9 and 10). After a brief pause, Martin, in response, initiates repair (line 12). Martin's repair displays his problem with Julia's turn. Specifically, Martin's partial repeat of Julia's turn, i.e., *nicht so gern,?* 'rather not,?' indicates that he has difficulty specifically with Julia's preference of not taking her car. Note also that by expressing her wish to not take her car, Julia doesn't leave Martin any other choice but to offer his car instead. In response to Martin's repair initiation, Julia provides an explanation for her wish, namely the fact that her car leaks oil (line 13). Martin in turn offers that they take his car (line 15). Schegloff (1984) notes that in their utterances, speakers display their understanding of what the prior turn was doing. By offering that they take his car, Martin reveals his understanding of Julia's utterances in lines 9, 10 and 13 as a pre-request and thus provides an offer of the projected request (i.e., taking his car instead). Furthermore, by expressing the lack of availability of her car and providing an account for her turn, Julia successfully elicits an offer from her co-participant rather than explicitly requesting that they take his car. In line 16, she accepts Martin's offer.

Martin's offer-turn is to be understood with reference to the interactional environment in which it is produced. In particular, it seems that the context in which Julia provides a reason for not wanting to take her car conditions a particular relevant next action, which is an offer. Furthermore, it is Martin's offer-turn that displays his understanding of Julia's account as a pre-request projecting a request sequence. In this segment, we can observe that Julia's account turn is understood by Martin as a pre-request not only due to its syntax and semantics, but also due to its sequential placement in the conversation.

The next data segment is another example of how an account serves as a pre-request. This is a telephone conversation between Dora and her mother. Dora, who is on an exchange program in the United States, is talking to her mother, who lives in Germany. In lines 10 and 11, Dora gives an account of why she has not yet purchased a cellular phone. Dora's account is produced in a context in which the conversation has been about her mother's new cell phone and a description of all the features that it has (not included in the data segment), and that they saved a congratulatory message on it for Dora's sister, Carla. It is in this sequential context that Dora explains why she hasn't bought one yet.

(3)   Dora/Mutti (Handy)

```
01    Mutti: [(    ) gspeichert  für die carla?
              [(    ) saved        for the carla?
              [(    ) saved for carla?

02    Dora : hm hm
              hm hm
              hm hm
```

```
03     Mutti:    herzlichen glückwunsch      zum  handy?=
                 from heart congratulations  to   cell phone=
                 congratulations on the cell phone=


04     Dora :    =he he   [he
                 =he he   [he
                 =he he   [he
                          [
05     Mutti:    [he he [he
                 [he he [he
                 [he he [he
                 [
06     Dora :    [he he he .hhhh  hm. gut.  he=
                 [he he he .hhhh  hm. good. he=
                 [he he he .hhh   hm. good. He=


07     Mutti:    =(    ) ham  wer abends gemacht?
                 =(    ) have we  night  done?
                 =(    ) we did it the other night?


08     Dora :    hm hm hm
                 hm hm hm
                 hm hm hm


09     Mutti :   und die (    )
                 and the (    )
                 and the (    )


10 -> Dora :     hm hm na    sicher .hh na   ich hätt    hier ein
                 hm hm well sure  .hh well i   have SBJ here a
                 hm hm well sure  .hh well i   would have had to


11 -> Dora :     vertrag   abschliessen müssen und das  wär
                 contract PRX+close      must   and that wasSBJ
                 sign a contract and that would have been


12 -> Dora :     mir zu    teuer  ge[wesen
                 me  too  expensive [been
                 too       expensive [for me
                                    [
13 -> Mutti :    [(      ) das handy  do:
                 [(      ) that   cell phone you:
                 [(      ) that cell phone you:


14 -> Dora :     hm=
                 hm=
                 hm=


15 -> Mutti :    =das  kriegst du amol   (.)  das   läuft zwar
                 =that get    you a time (.) that  runs  MP
                 =you're gonna get that one some time(.)it runs


16 -> Mutti :    jetzt auf mei nomen und auf unser bank
                 now   on  my  name  and on  our   bank
                 now   on  my  name  and on  our   bank
```

```
17 -> Mutti :   [konto
                [account
                [account
                [

18     Dora :   [hm hm hm
                [hm hm hm
                [hm hm hm

19     Mutti:   weil    es anders net zu machen ging?
                because it other  not to do      went?
                because it wouldn't have gone otherwise?

20     Dora :   hm hm hm=
                hm hm hm=
                hm hm hm=

21     Mutti:   aber  wenns du   haam kimst du    brauchst   aa 'n
                but   when  you home come +you need          also a
                but   when  you come home you  also need   a

22     Mutti:   telefon   unterwegs  oder sonst was und-
                telephone on the way or   other      and-
                telephone on the way or   something like that and-

23              (0.1)

24 -> Dora  :   jo::    na   gott nehm isch    dann he he he
                yeah::  well god  take i+it    then he he he
                yeah::  well god  i'll take it then he he he

25 -> Dora  :   des  is nett        he he he
                that is nice         he he he
                that's  nice of you he he he
```

After a repair sequence (lines 13 and 14), Dora's mother offers her cellular phone to Dora when she goes back home (line 15). Note that the offer is produced in response to Dora's account (lines 10–12). After some insert expansions (lines 16–22), Dora accepts her mother's offer (line 24). Similar to the previous data segment, an account is heard by its recipient as a pre-request. And again we observe how an account, due to its sequential placement in talk, is understood by its recipient as a pre-request, and how its recipient, in turn, orients to the account as a pre-request by offering the projected request.

It has been observed that accounts regularly accompany rejections to offers, invitations and requests and that their placement and "no fault" quality are related to matters of face (Heritage 1984a; Levinson 1983). Heritage (1984a) argues that accounts that express a lack of ability to perform the preferred next action generally enable social solidarity (272–273). In segment 2 and 3, the account turns do not accompany a dispreferred response, but instead describe a situation in which speakers have trouble accessing an object (either because of its malfunctioning or its high price). In response, the recipients offer the object that the speakers have trouble accessing. In doing so, they display affiliation with their co-participant and thus enhance social solidarity.

3.2.3   Pre-requests in some other possible turn-formats

Pre-requests may also have other turn designs. For example, likes/dislikes, or one's wishes may be also understood by a recipient as pre-requests. Similar to the pre-request turns in the previous segments, it is their sequential placement in the talk that makes them hearable as pre-requests. The next segment demonstrates how in specific interactional environments, the speaker's expression of likes is produced such that it serves as a pre-request. It also becomes apparent that a turn performs a pre-request when its recipient, in turn, demonstrably orients to it as projecting a request sequence. In this example, the pre-request turn-format is mentioning one's likes. This is a conversation between Markus and his grand-mother. In the following excerpt, Markus's grandmother explains to him that she asked her neighbor (Susi) for a couple of apricots while she was visiting her the night before (lines 1–2) and that Susi brought her some apricots that noon (line 3), so she can bake an apricot cake for Nicki (Markus's sister) since she likes it so much (lines 1–6). Upon hearing this information, Markus mentions that he likes apricot cake as well (line 7).

(4)   Oma/Markus (Aprikosenkuchen)

```
01    Oma   :                              [und   da      war
                                           [and   there   was
                                           [and   i       was

02    Oma   : ich gestern    abend    mal  bei der susi ob  sie nicht nicht not
              i   yesterday   evening once  at  the susi whether she not
              yesterday at susi's whether she has any any couple and

03    Oma   : ein paar    hat und  da     hat  sie mir heut   mittag so ne
              a   couple  has and there   have she me  today  noon    such
              there she handed me a bowl today through

04    Oma   : schüssel vom ähm ähm hier am fenster (.) reingegeben
              a bowl     of uhm uhm here at window  (.) gave
              uhm uhm the window (.) now i'll bake then

05    Oma   : da     mach ich dann  morgen    nen aprokosenkuchen:hh die
              there make I   then  tomorrow  an  apricot   cake   :hh the
              tomorrow an apricot cake :hh nicki likes
```

```
06     Oma   : nicki isst ja so gerne aprikosenkuchen=
                nicki eats yea so like   apricot  cake=
                eating  that   so much=

07 -> Markus: =ja   ich  auch.
               =yes  me   too.
               =yes  me   too.

08 -> Oma   : du    auch?=
               you   too?=
               you   too?=

09 -> Markus: =ja
               =yes
               =yes

10 ->          (0.2)

11 -> Markus: [hehe-
              [hehe-
              [hehe-
              [
12 -> Oma   : [hehe(.) ja    den  kann ich dir   leider         nicht
              [hehe(.) yes   that can  i   you   unfortunately not
              [hehe (.) yes i unfortunately can't mail that to

13 -> Oma   : schicken=
               send=
               you=

13    Markus : =.hhhh ja,  kannst  einfrieren hehe  gibst der nicki
               =.hhhh yes, can+you PRX+freeze hehe  give  the nicki
               =.hhh  yes, you can freeze it  hehe  give      nicki

14    Markus : nur   ein  stück hehehe
               only  one  piece hehehe
               only  one  piece hehehe
```

In line 7, Markus expresses to his grandmother that he likes apricot cake as well. This is followed by his grandmother's "try-marked" turn expressing her surprise (line 8). After a pause (line 10), some laughter and a micro pause, Markus's grandmother explains that she cannot mail him an apricot cake (line 12). In fact, her turn provides an account for not offering to bake him a cake since he lives in the US. Note that by providing a reason for her failure, Markus's grandmother displays that she took Markus's turn as a pre-request. In other words, the grandmother's turn shows her understanding of the sequential context, what the relevant next is and that what she is doing is something else.

In sum, the above discussion of sequential organization of pre-requests in everyday German has illustrated that:

a) Utterances such as questions (segment 1), accounts (segments 2 and 3) and mentioning one's likes (segment 4) are mobilized as an interactional device to facilitate the projection of a dispreferred action-type (i.e., a request);

b) The placement of such turn formats in the talk, in combination with their composition, contributes to their interpretation as a pre-request; and

c) Recipients demonstrably orient to these turn formats as pre-requests and provide, in turn, the next preferred action (i.e., an offer, or in some cases an explanation for their failure to perform such an action).

3.3. Request turn designs in relation to their pre-requests and their subsequent talk

The above section illustrated that the action of pre-request gets accomplished by virtue of its composition in combination with its sequential placement and participation within sequences of talk. It was also noted that pre-requests are affiliative interactional devices which are designed in such a way as to "elicit" an offer and consequently to avoid making a request. A request, however, may be produced if a pre-emptive offer is not possible. In such instances, the important interactional work that pre-requests seem to accomplish is that their outcome and their subsequent expansion may not only motivate speakers to produce the first pair part of a request, but may also influence the composition and type of a request.

The following section offers a description of a selection of such instances. In particular, the focus will be on a request type produced in an interactional environment in which a pre-request fails to elicit an offer from its recipient, and in which its subsequent talk reveals some conditionality upon the request grant. Speakers orient to the conditionality of the request grant in the way they construct their request turn, specifically by incorporating the conditional *wenn*-clause (if-clause) as a component of the request first pair part in order to express the conditionality of their request. The following section will provide a detailed description of such an instance of request which I call *contingent request*. First, however, let us review some literature on conditional clauses in English and German, with a focus on the studies which have looked at the usage of *wenn*-clauses in spoken discourse.

3.3.1 Conditional if-clauses: Their structure and function in English and German

Within linguistics, conditional clauses have received much attention (Dancygier 1993; Dancygier and Sweetser 1996; Dancygier and Sweetser 2000; Sweetser 1990). Such studies have described four main characteristics of conditional if-clauses in English, namely: (1) conditionals consist of a complex sentence which is composed of a main clause or an *apodosis* (q) and a subordinate clause or a *protasis* (p) which are connected by a conditional conjunction *if*; (2) conditional clauses contain subjunctive and indicative verb forms; (3) the subordinate clause and the main clause have a relation such that the main clause cannot be uttered without the "prior assumption" of the subordinate clause; and (4) the "*if p, then q*" clause order refers to the sequence and realization of events. In other words, the *protasis* offers the background or condition for the realization of the event described in the *apodosis*. However, reversed order is possible in a conversation. Furthermore, it has been suggested that occurrences of conditional if-clauses in spoken discourse are closely related to contexts and speakers' participations in the conversation (Ford and Thompson 1986; Ford 1993; Ford 1997). For example, English speakers seem to use conditional *if*-clauses as resources to deal with and manage interactionally "delicate" situations in which politeness and face might be of the speaker's concern. This understanding may have to do with the hypotheticality and optionality contained in conditionals which allow speakers to mitigate potentially dispreferred interactional moves. In her examination of conditional *if*-clauses in everyday conversation, Ford (1997) states that interactants treat "their content as provisional, less than certain; an alternative is always implicitly acknowledged" (389). In general, *if*-clauses seem to occur in conversations whenever issues of "face" are at play (397).

Studies on conditional *wenn*-clauses in German conversation suggest a similar relationship between main and subordinate clauses, and propose that German speakers also utilize the conditional *wenn*-clause with its hypotheticality and optionality as a politeness strategy (Auer 2000; Günthner 1999b). Furthermore, these studies have shown that similar to English if-clauses in spoken discourse, German *wenn*-clauses may also frequently occur in the initial position of a sentence. However, the initial position of German *wenn*-clauses may be tightly integrated into the syntactic structure of the following main-clause (Günthner 1999b; Auer 2000). In other words, the initial position of the *wenn*-clause entails structural changes in that the following main clause must then begin with the main clause finite verb. For example (translation is mine):

```
wenn sie=n JOB haben  wollen, (.) müssen  sie=n bisschen da     aufn PUNKT
if   you=a JOB have    want,   (.) must    you=a little   thereto the POINT
if   you= want to have a job, (.) you have to get a little bit to the

kommen
get
POINT
```

(Auer 2000: 174; my translation)

In addition, Auer notes that the initial position of *wenn*-clauses is related to "speech-acts". According to Auer, speakers position *wenn*-clauses initially in order to mitigate a face threatening act. He provides the following example of an interruption (translation is mine):

```
wenn ich (-) grad WEIter    ausführen   darf;  (0.5) Sie wissen ja    in de: in
if   i   (-) just CONtinue elaborate   may;   (0.5) You know    MP    in th: in
if   I   (-) may  just      elaborate;         (0.5) You know    that in in

der AUtoinsdustrie .h herrschen       sehr große k´konkuRENZ,    markt
the CAr industry   .h exist           very big  c'competition, market
the CAr industry   .h there exists very big  c'competition, market
```

(Auer 2000: 181; my translation)

By uttering the *wenn*-clause in the front-position, German speakers may perform a face threatening act, such as in the above example. These studies, however, provide only an analysis of the syntax of conditional *wenn*-clauses in German discourse; they fail to discuss the interactional function of conditional *wenn*-clauses in everyday conversation, i.e., how they are instantiated within talk-in-interaction. One environment in which conditional *wenn*-clauses occur is the contingent requests turn. The following section provides a description of instances of contingent requests which contain a conditional *wenn*-clause.

3.3.2 Contingent request turn: Conditional wenn-clause in the initial position

Data segment 5 shows a speaker producing a projected request, even though hedging responses to its pre-request had indicated the request to be problematic in some way. A conditional *wenn*-clause is produced immediately before the actual request phrase; this *wenn*-clause displays the requester's orientation to the problematicity of the request. Furthermore, this *wenn*-clause expresses the contingency of granting his request. In the excerpt Thomas, who is on an exchange program in America, is talking to his friend, Mark, in Germany. This conversation occurs a few days before Mark's trip to the U.S. During their conversation, Thomas asks his friend to find and bring a few pictures of him (Thomas) when he had long hair.

    (5) Thomas/Mark (Fotos)

```
01->1a Thomas : FOTO    is a gutes  stichwort genau.   .hh hast du
                PICTURE is a good   keyword   exactly. .hh have you
                PICUTRE is a good   keyword   exactly. .hh do you still

02->1a Thomas : noch  fotos       von   mir mit langen haarn?
                still pictures     from  me  with long   hair?
                have  any pictures of    me  with long   hair?

03              (1.0)
```

```
04      Markus : äh:m
                 uh:m
                 uh:m

05             (1.0)

06      Markus : wenn: (1.0)
                 if:    (1.0)
                 if:    (1.0)

07      Thomas : dann
                 then
                 then

08->1b  Markus : ja  es ich jetz    sag ich mal .hh  diese schwabenparty
                 yes it i   now      say i   MP  .hh  these swabian party
                 yes it now i wanna  say         .hh  these swabian party

09      Markus : photos
                 pictures
                 pictures

10->1c  Thomas : aha da     [hab  i  aber
                 uhu there  [have i  but
                 uhu but   i[have
                            [
11->1b  Markus : [die   könnt ich scho     finden
                 [them  could i   already  find
                 [i     could     actually find them

12->1c  Thomas : da      hab  ich aber    keine richtigen langen
                 there   have i   but     not   right     long
                 but in those i   really  don't have      long

13      Thomas : ha  [are
                 ha  [ir
                 ha  [ir
                     [

14      Markus : [da      hast  nich    richtig lange haare
                 [there   have you not  right   long  hair
                 [you     don't have    really  long  hair on them

15->2a  Thomas : und  sonst      haste    keine       fotos      von mir oder?
                 and  otherwise  have+you no          pictures   of  me  or?
                 and  otherwise  you          don't have any pictures of me  right?

16->2b  Markus : soll   ich mal schaun  quasi?
                 shall  i   MP  look    indeed so to speak?
                 you want me     to look for them?

17      Thomas : ((cough))
```

```
18      Markus : [(  )prin]
                 [(  )prin]
                 [(  )prin]
                 [           ]
19->2c Thomas : [schau mal]
                 [look MP  ]
                 [take a look]


20      Markus : prinzipiell: (0.5) [naja.]
                 in principl:e (0.5) [well.]
                 in principl:e (0.5) [well.]
                                     [   ]
21      Thomas :                     [wasch] wahrscheinlich eher    nich ne
                                      [prob]  probably        rather not  right
                                      [prob]  probably        rather not  right


22      Thomas : weil    du [hast] ja ziem-
                 because you [have] MP rath-
                 because you [have] rath-
                              [    ]
23      Markus :              [wir ]
                              [we  ]
                              [we  ]


24      Markus : wir ham         ziemlich wenich geknippst    ir [gendwie
                 we  have         rather   few    photographed som[ehow
                 we somehow took rather   few                    pict[ures
                                                                 [
25      Thomas :                                              [ziemlich  wenig
                                                              [rather    few
                                                              [we took   rather
26      Thomas : fotos        von mir gmacht ne,=
                 pictures     of  me  made right,=
                 few pictures of  me  right,=


27      Markus : =joa
                 =yea
                 =yea


28->3a Thomas : .hhh wennst irgendwas findest könnst      es mitbringen
                 .hhh if you anything  find+you could+you  it PRX+bring
                 .hhh if you find anything you   could bring it along


29      Thomas : weil    äh die eva die ä:h   unterrichtet a⁴deutsch und
                 because uh the eva who u:h  teaches also      german and
                 because uh eva who a:h also teaches          german and studies


30      Thomas : studiert hier und ha(h)t irgendwie gmeint das  würd  sie
                 studies  here and ha(h)s somehow   said   that would she
                 here and kind of said that she would actually be


31      Thomas : scho    interessieren.hhh
                 already interest.hhh
                 interested in.hhh
```

```
32      Markus : aha
                 uhu
                 uhu

33      Thomas : wie ich denn      so           mit  langen haaren ausseh
                 whati  actually so              with long    hair  PRX+looked
                 whati  actually looked like with long     hair

34      Markus : ja
                 ja
                 ja

35->4a  Thomas : genau   und wenn du    da     was        hast  kannst    mir  halt
                 exactly and if  you   there anything  have  can+you   me   MP
                 exactly and if  you   have  any there  you   can also  maybe

36->4a  Thomas : da   a: irgendwie e' foto oder zwei mitbringen
                 there also somehow a  picture or  two PRX+bring
                 bring me a picture or two

37               (0.5)

38      Thomas : ((sniff))

39->4b  Markus : no     kloar ich hab's mir  mal  notiert     sozusagen
                 yea    clear i   have+it RP MP  note        so to say
                 yea sure    i    made a         note of it so to speak

40->4c  Thomas :  oke:    alles       klar
                 oka:y  everything clear
                 oka:y  got you
```

The request sequence begins with Thomas' pre-request (lines 1–2), projecting the production of a base action, namely a request. Thomas' use of *noch* 'still' in his inquiry displays his understanding that Mark, at some point, must have had pictures of Thomas with long hair. And it is Mark's response that may or may not lead to the production of a request. Mark, in turn, suggests pictures from the Swabian party (line 8) and offers to look for them (line 11). This, however, is delivered with some hesitation and delay (lines 3, 4, 5, and 6): after a pause, Mark initiates his turn with the lexical item *wenn* 'if', but does not continue the turn. After a pause of one second, Thomas comes in and utters *dann* 'then' (line 7), thus displaying his projection of the second part of an "if X then Y" compound turn constructional type. According to Lerner (1991), due to their construction, completion of such compound TCUs may be anticipated by the next speaker since their initial component projects the location and the form of their final component (307). By producing the resumptive element *dann*, Thomas displays his understanding of the location of the final component of the compound TCU, even though the *wenn*-component has not yet been completed. Similar to Mark, Thomas does not complete his turn. In brief, by producing the initial element in a *wenn-dann*-construction, both speakers orient to some possible conditionality related to Thomas' pre-request.

Mark's offer, however, fails since it turns out that Thomas did not have long hair in those pictures (line 12). One key job of pre-requests is to explore whether there are obstacles to granting the request (Schegloff in press). The subsequent turns to the pre-request (at arrows "1b" and "1c") display that there are some problems with Thomas' projectable request. At this point in the conversation, possible moves include either withholding the projectable request, articulating it despite the hedging, or producing another pre-request. And as we can see, the conversation continues with a repetition of basically the same pre-sequence: following Mark's offer rejection, Thomas raises the possibility of other pictures (line 15), which receives another offer from Mark (line 16). Note that Mark's second offer is designed in question format, which given the circumstances could be interpreted as questioning the second pre-request, i.e., the potential difficulty of finding those pictures. At this point, Thomas could reject Mark's offer, thereby acknowledging the trouble that finding those particular pictures may cause his friend. However, he accepts his friend's offer (line 19). To reiterate, a pre-request is produced (at the "1a" arrows), followed by an offer (at the "1b" arrows), which is rejected (at the "1c" arrows). This is followed by a repetition of the same sequence type, i.e., a pre-request (at the "2a" arrow), and a subsequent offer (at the "2b" arrow), which is however followed by an acceptance (at the "2c" arrow). In addition, this exchange reveals a potential conditionality of Mark's offer.

The conversation continues with some additional talk related to the pre-request sequence. This talk is initiated by Mark and contains elements which may be understood as Mark's possible inability to perform his offer. Mark begins his turn with the lexical item *prinzipiell*: 'in principle', thus indicating his general positive attitude towards fulfilling his friend's projectable request. However, he continues his turn with a pause and *naja* 'well' – elements which may occur in dispreferred turns (Auer and Uhmann 1982; Pomerantz 1984). Thomas projects his friend's possible dispreferred turn and aligns himself by mentioning the probability of finding any pictures. This is followed by a collaborative agreement of both friends on the fact that they took so few pictures (lines 21–27). The pre-requests and the following talk indicate some contingency on Mark's offer, i.e., he must find/have the pictures in order to be able to bring them along. Considering this circumstance, three interactional moves may be projectable: (1) Thomas withholds his request and tells his friend to forget about it; (2) he asks his friend to bring some pictures along anyhow; or (3) he produces a "contingent request", i.e., he makes a request upon the condition that his friend finds the pictures. As we saw, Thomas articulates a contingent request even though his projected request had been rendered problematic by hedging responses to his pre-requests (at arrow "3a").

Thomas' contingent request turn is composed of a subordinate clause introduced by the conditional conjunction *wenn* and a main clause. The way Thomas composes his *wenn*-clause displays features of "recipient design" (Schegloff 1980). In other words, Thomas' *wenn*-clause is designed in such a way as to display his orientation to features uttered by the recipient of the request (Mark) in a previous turn (line 11), i.e., the condition for the request to be complied, namely finding the pictures. Furthermore, speakers may display affiliation with their prior speaker by constructing their current turn similarly to the way their prior speaker's utterance was composed (Goldberg 1978). And indeed in this data segment, by incorporating elements from Mark's prior turn into his conditional *wenn*-clause, Thomas affiliates on the syntactic and thematic levels with Mark's prior turn.

Note that Thomas continues his turn and provides an account for his request (lines 28–33) which receives minimal responses from Mark (lines 32 and 34). When Thomas' contingent request fails to engender a response action from his recipient (acceptance or rejection of granting the request), he tries again and repeats his request (at the "4a" arrows). His second request is formulated in a format similar to his first request, i.e., it also contains a *wenn*-clause which refers to the contingency of possessing pictures. This is, then, followed by an acceptance to comply with the request (arrow "4b") and the sequence closure (arrow "4c").

Both conditional *wenn*-clauses in Thomas' request-turns occur before the main clause – a commonly found position for conditional *wenn*-clauses in spoken German (Auer 2000: 179). In her analysis of *if*-clauses in spoken English, Ford (1997) states that the initial position of speaker's *if*-clauses may show the "relevance of current turn to previous talk" (403). The same holds true for the present German data: the initial position of the requester's (Thomas') *wenn*-clause connects it thematically to the immediate previous talk (the fact that there are a few pictures which have to be found). In addition, the turn-initial position of the conjunction *wenn* may project an expanded turn shape and thus postpone the next possible turn-transition place – a feature which has also been observed in English "if X then Y" turn constructions (Lerner 1991). By initiating the request turn with a *wenn*-clause, the speaker shows his recipient that some additional turn-constructional components (e.g., the request) may be following and may thereby delay the next possible turn-transition place.

Thomas' request turn is a compound TCU in an "if X then Y" format (Lerner 1996a).[5] The initial position of the subordinate *wenn*-clause and its content allow the projection of a "unit-type" (Sacks et al. 1974), i.e., a request. In other words, in combination with the subsequent turn-initial placement of the subordinate clause, the sequential context (i.e., the pre-request) may project an upcoming request. Note also that Mark's incomplete *wenn* construction, in line 6, and Thomas' incomplete *dann* construction may contribute to the request projection.

In other words, by producing the *wenn*-clause first, Thomas delays the production of the request (thereby orienting to its dispreferred status). In addition, the actual request is delayed not by just anything, but by an element that allows for the projection of the upcoming requesting action. Thomas thus orients in two ways to the dispreferredness of the turn (moreover, he gives Mark the chance to co-produce the utterance).

In brief, the above analysis demonstrates how a pre-request sequence and its expansion shape up the resulted contingent request. A contingent request may contain a conditional *wenn*-clause which may be a realization of the contingent circumstances which have been revealed in the pre-request and its expansion. In addition, the example illustrates that the initial position of the conditional *wenn*-clause in the request turn may have to do with preference organization.

3.3.3   Contingent request turn: conditional wenn-clause in mid position

A *wenn*-clause in a contingent request turn may be positioned in the middle of the request TCU. Similar to the previous example, the contingent request turn contains a conditional *wenn*-clause which addresses some conditionality upon the request compliance (a matter that was mentioned earlier in the talk). Following is a conversation between Markus, a German graduate student at an American university, who calls his sister, Nicki, in Germany. This conversation occurs shortly after Markus has returned to the US from a visit to Germany. The conversation topic prior to the request sequence has concerned the low price of the sweatshirt (compared to the price of the same sweatshirt in Germany) that Markus has recently bought his sister in the U.S.

(6)   Markus/Nicki (Sweatshirt)

```
01     Nicki   : und hattste eigentlich nochma son      t-shirt gesichtet  so
                 and had+you actually   again  such+a t-shirt seen         such
                 and had you actually   seen    such a t-shirt again       like

02     Nicki   : wie  ichs mir  was       vorstell?
                 like i+it RP  something  imagine?
                 the  ones i              imagine?

03     Markus  : ne: .hh also so oft    geh ich da    ja    au    nisch hin
                 no: .hh well so often  go  i   there MP    also  not   there
                 no: .hh well I don't   go       there that often

04     Nicki   : ja
                 yes
                 yes
```

```
05    Markus : ((snief)) und ich hab      da      gekuckt aber die  ab  als ich
               ((snief)) and i   have     there   looked  but they bu  when i
               ((sniff)) and i   looked   there but       they but    when i also

06    Markus : auch eure sweat shirts gekauft hab  .hh und dann als
               also your sweat shirts bought  have .hh and then when
               bought your sweat shirts .hh and then when i uhm was

07    Markus : isch ähm mim   john da    war  sein computer umtauschen (3.0)
               i    uhm with  john there was  his  computer exchange   (3.0)
               there     with john exchanging his  computer (3.0) and uh

08    Markus : unt äh da     hab  isch aber nur    die sweat shirts wieder
               and uh there  have i    but  only   the sweat shirts again
               but i only saw the sweat shirts there again und for for

09    Markus : gesehn und an an    t-shirts is halt jetzt
               seen   and for for  t-shirts is just now
               t-shirts it's just not

10    Nicki  : na    klar
               yea   clear
               yea   sure

11    Markus : nich die  zeit
               not  the  time
               the       time now

12    Nicki  : jaja
               yes yes
               yes yes

13    Markus : .hh [und] wenn die   dann
               .hh [and] when they  then
               .hh [and] when they  then
                   [   ]
14    Nicki  : [( )]findest     hab ich  halt pech     gehabt
               [( )]find+   you have i   just bad luck had
               [( )]you find        i    just had tough luck

15    Markus : und  was da war das war halt so äh (.) .hh so ps hhh des des
               and  what there was that was just so uh (.) so ps hhh it it
               and  what was there that was just so uh (.) so ps hhh it it

16    Markus:  sah       so komisch aus (1.0) da    da    war nix      da    war
               looked    so strange PRX (1.0) there there was nothing there was
               it looked so strange     (1.0) there there was nothing there

17    Markus : halt     zu der zeit nix      vielleicht .hhh kommt dann in in
               MP   just at that time nothing maybe      .hhh comes MP    in in
               was  just at that time nothing maybe      .hhh it will come

18    Markus : paar  wochen wenn ma    wieder mal hinfahrn
               a few weeks  when once  again MP   PTX+drive
               in in a few  weeks when we go there again
```

```
19    Markus : .hhh und dann ähm
               .hhh and then uhm
               .hhh then uhm


20 -> Nicki  : was  du   noch (.)  was   du  noch kucken kannst    wenn du kein
               what you  still(.)  what  you still look  can+you   if   you no
               what you  still(.)  what  youstillcan look for    if  you


21 -> Nicki  : t-shirt .hh kriegst (1.0) ich vermute du   wirst      keins
               t-shirt .hh get      (1.0) i   guess   you will+you   none
               don't find .hh a t-shirt (1.0) i guess you won't get any


22 -> Nicki  : kriegn weil    des einfach keine zeit dafür is aber (.)  du
               get    because it simply  no    time for+it is but  (.)  you
               because it's simply not the time for it but (.) you


23 -> Nicki  : könntest ma (3.0)  nach nem schönen (2.0) ähm  wenn de
               could    MP (3.0)  for  a   pretty  (2.0) uhm  if   you
               could    (3.0) for a pretty (2.0) uhm if you have time


24 -> Nicki  : zeit hast (.)  ähm (.)  nach nem jeans hemd  kucken (1.0)
               time have (.)  uhm (.)  for  a   jeans shirt look   (1.0)
               (.)  uhm (.)  look for a jeans shirt (1.0) long    sleeves


25 -> Nicki  : lange ärmel  (.)  und (2.0)  in nem in nem satten dunklen
               long  sleeves(.)  and (2.0)  in a  in a  rich   dark
               (.)and (2.0) in a in a rich dark


26    Nicki  : jeans blau
               jeans blue
               jeans blue


26             (2.0)


27    Markus : hmhm
               mhm
               mhm


28    Nicki  : weil     des  was  ich mir  vor drei  jahrn bei dir gekauft
               because that what i   ago      three years at  you bought
               because  the  one  i   bought when visiting you three years


29    Nicki  : hab (.)des  is noch  einwandfrei des lieb ich auch über
               have(.)that is still perfect      it  love i    also over
               ago (.)thatis still  perfect i love it over everything i


30    Nicki  : alles       nur  ich mein des  is seit drei  jahren getragen und
               everything just i    mean that is for  three years   worn     and
               just mean it's been worn for three years and it's not


31    Nicki  : so richtig äh (.)  n dunkles blau is des  nicht mehr oder
               so really  uh (.)  a dark     blue is that not    more or
               really uh (.) dark blue or (.) like really any
```

```
32    Nicki  : (.) son   richtiges jeansblau weiste  [(son)  ]
                 (.) such really    jeansblue know+you [(such a)]
                 longer jeans blue you know          [(such a)]
                                                     [
33    Markus :                                       [aja dann]
                                                     [oh yea then]
                                                     [oh yea then]

34    Markus : färbs doch ein
                 dye it MP PRX
                 just dye it

35           (1.0)

36    Nicki  : he?
                 hu?
                 hu?

37    Markus : da färbs doch ein
                 there dye it MP PRX
                 just dye it

38           (2.0)

39    Nicki  : (herin) (.) das  mach ich nicht wegen    son    jeans hemd
                 (in it) (.) that make i    not   because of such a jeans  shirt
                 (in it) (.) i won't do that for such a jeans shirt (.)

40    Nicki  : (.) die   kriegste heut  schon billiger  als die farbe
                 (.) them  get+you  today even  cheaper   as  the dye
                 you get them nowadays even cheaper than the dye

41    Nicki  : beinah
                 almost
                 almost

42    Markus : hehe
                 he he
                 he he

43 -> Nicki  : also  isch ( ) aber (2.0) wenn de     damal was sehn
                 so   i    ( ) but  (2.0) if   there MP something see
                 so   i    ( ) but  (2.0) if   you    should see something there

44 -> Nicki  : solltest was      (.) ganz    nett aussieht  irgendwie oder
                 should  something (.) totally neat  looks like somehow   or
                 something that looks really neat somehow or and if not

42 -> Nicki  : und wenn nicht is au   nicht schlimm aber .hhh da     kannst
                 and if   not  is also not  bad     but  .hhh then   can
                 it's also okay but .hhh then you can

43    Nicki  : du   das   kaufen
                 you  it   buy
                 buy it

44           (1.0)
```

```
45    Markus :    mhm (1.0) [jaja (.) ma     kucken    ]
                  mhm (1.0) [yea yea (.)MP  see        ]
                  mhm (1.0) [yea yea (.) we'll see     ]
                            [                          ]
46    Nicki  :              [(gähn)                    ]
                            [(yawn)                    ]

47           (1.0)

48    Markus : oje:
               oh:
               oh:
```

Prior to the request base adjacency pair (line 20–25), Markus and his sister, Nicki, have been talking about the sweatshirt Markus has bought her from an American wholesale store with low-priced products. Nicki expresses her surprise and excitement about the sweatshirt's low price several times (not in the transcript). Following this, she produces a pre-request (lines 1–2). The adverb *nochma* 'again' in Nicki's inquiry displays that Markus has brought her T-shirts from the US in the past. Markus, in turn, responds to his sister's inquiry negatively and provides two accounts for not having bought any T-shirts for her, namely that he does not go to that store frequently (line 3), and that it is not the season for T-shirts yet (lines 9–11). Note that in his explanation, Markus mentions the reasons he was at the store (lines 6–7). In doing so, he justifies the last two times he was at this store, signaling that he does not frequently go there, and that he did not go there on his own behalf. He does, however, offer to his sister to look for T-shirts some time (line 17–18) but makes it clear that he will not go out of his way to do so. Markus's TCU contains the adverb *mal* 'once', signaling no specific time for going to that store. Similar to the previous example, the pre-request and its expansion reveal certain contingencies for the projected request to be granted. In this datum, the contingencies seem to be time-related, i.e., the frequency of going to that store and the season for T-shirts.

Following Markus's offer, Nicki produces a contingent request (20–25). Note that Nicki is requesting something new - something other than a T-shirt. However, the requested object will not be mentioned until later in the turn. Similar to Thomas' contingent request in the previous data segment, Nicki's request turn contains a conditional *wenn*-clause (lines 20 and 21) which also realizes the conditional circumstances (viz. the possibility of not finding a T-shirt) which came up during the pre-expansion. Nicki's *wenn*-clause is followed by a pause (line 21). When looking at her turn, one might expect her request to come next, i.e., that she name the object that she is requesting. However, Nicki continues her turn by expressing her assumption that Martin will probably not find any T-shirts and repeats the account that Markus had given earlier, namely that it is just not the season for them (line 21–22). In doing so, Nicki displays her alignment with her brother on the account that he had given earlier. She continues her turn by contrasting her old request with an alternative one (she used the conjunction "aber" 'but' in her turn), namely a jeans shirt (23–25). Note that right at the point in her utterance where the requested object should be mentioned, she produces a conditional *wenn*-clause through which she expresses the circumstance under which she wishes/expects her request to be granted, i.e., only if her brother has the time. Note also that in his response to Nicki's pre-request, Markus had uttered the adverb *oft* 'often'. So far, Nicki has produced two *wenn*-clauses in her request turn, each referring to one of the contingencies brought up during the pre-expansion (the season for T-shirts and the time for going to the store). After a brief pause she utters the requested object, namely a jeans shirt. The jeans shirt specifications are produced in increments after pauses.

Similar to the previous excerpt, the position of the *wenn*-clauses here suggests that they are performing some interactional work. Both *wenn*-clauses in this segment are produced in mid-turn position, that is, the speaker first articulates a portion of the request but inserts a *wenn*-clause before completing the request turn. In doing so, Nicki delays the next possible turn transition space and the turn constructional component that delivers the request. This could be understood as a device through which Nicki postpones the delivery of her dispreferred action, i.e., a request. Following Nicki's request, there is a pause at a position in which the next action is relevant, namely either agreeing to grant the request or rejecting it. Markus produces a continuer (line 27) upon which Nicki gives an account for her request of a jeans shirt from this particular store (line 28–32). The next relevant action for Markus is to either agree to grant his sister's request or to reject it. As we note, however, Markus in turn suggests an alternative action on his sister's part which may indicate that he is looking for a way out of complying with the request. In response, Nicki initiates "open" class repair (Drew 1997) which displays her difficulty with the prior turn (line 36). Drew notes that "open" class repair initiators occur in response to turns which may appear not to be sequentially appropriate next to prior turns. Considering Nicki's prior turns in which she expresses a request and provides an account for her request, Markus's suggestion about dyeing her old jeans shirt seems sequentially not appropriate. Markus repeats his suggestion (i.e., the repairable turn) upon which Nicki produces a counterargument (lines 39–41). Nicki's turn serves to uphold her request which can be observed in her next turn: here, she produces another contingent request turn which is formulated similarly to her previous request turn (including a *wenn*-clause). The contingency is if Markus sees something nice. Upon this last request by his sister, Markus finally agrees to comply with the action (line 45). However, his agreement is minimal. Following a continuer, a pause, *jaja* 'yea yea' and a micro pause, he says *ma kucken* 'we'll see'. In other words, he is postponing the decision whether or not to comply with his sister's request. In sum, this data segment exemplifies instances of contingent requests which are occasioned by reference to their pre-expansion. The contingent request turns contain three conditional *wenn*-clauses, through which speakers display to their co-participant their understanding and acknowledgement of the fact that their request compliance is contingent upon the recipient's ability and desire. Furthermore, similar to the previous data segment, the position of the *wenn*-clause in this example may also have to do with preference organization. As we noted in this datum, two of the *wenn*-clauses are positioned in the middle of the request turn, i.e., immediately after the initial components of the request turn and right before the requested object is articulated. The mid-position of the *wenn*-clauses may not only defer the production of a portion of the dispreferred action (i.e., the requested item), but also postpone the next possible turn-transition place. In doing so, the speaker mentions the contingency under which she wishes her request to be complied before the next possible transition space.

Another feature that these contingent request sequences share is their length. By just looking at the above excerpts we can immediately notice that the pre-requests, their expansions, and their occasioned contingent requests are accomplished through relatively long the stretches of talk. Actually, all request cases in my corpus in which the pre-request sequence signals some problems/contingencies with granting the projected request, are accomplished within several turns at talk.

3.4. Discussion

This chapter offered a detailed description of how speakers' contributions to conversations are oriented to the sequential context of the interaction; in other words, how each turn at talk is contextual, how the grammatical structure of each turn is shaped by the context of prior talk, and how each turn establishes a context to which the next turn will be oriented. The first part of this chapter explored pre-request turns in German. It was suggested that it is the sequential placement of turns in talk coupled with their linguistic composition which contributes to their recipient's interpretation as a pre-request. Three pre-request turn-formats were described:[6]

(1) Pre-requests may be designed as a question that explores the possibility of a projected request being granted (segment 1);

(2) Pre-requests may have the shape of an account of an action or lack of access to an object (segments 2 and 3); and

(3) Pre-requests can take the form of mentioning of likes (segment 4).

It was illustrated how speakers utilize these turn-formats as an interactional device to facilitate a projection of an action type, namely a request.

In the second half of the chapter, I showed that the production of requests and their turn shapes is closely connected to the local context and speakers' contributions. It was demonstrated how pre-requests and their expansions occasion the type of requests speakers make. Instances of "contingent requests" and their compositions were presented which showed that they are instantiated by the contingent circumstances which resulted during their pre-request expansions. One particular feature the exemplified contingent requests share is that they contain a conditional *wenn*-clause that may be a linguistic realization of the contingent circumstances. The analysis of the grammatical structure of contingent requests exemplified that the way a turn is designed displays the speaker's understanding of the sequential connection between prior turn and activities being managed in previous turns. In addition, it was illustrated that speakers affiliate with their co-participants on the syntactic as well as the thematic level by incorporating elements from their recipient's prior turn into their conditional *wenn*-clause.

An analysis of the position of the *wenn*-clause in a contingent request suggests that this may be related to preference organization. In other words, by inserting the *wenn*-clause in the initial or mid position of the request turn, speakers delay the delivery of the object or service they wish to request. This could be understood as a device which speakers utilize to deal with the dispreferred situation of producing the request despite the circumstances. Overall, the presented cases of contingent requests illustrated that not only the content and the composition of an utterance, but also its position within the turn are connected to the preference organization.

As noted earlier in this chapter, requests are dispreferred social activities. Speakers have resources such as pre-requests which are available to them to avoid such activities (Sacks 1996; Schegloff 1990). According to Goodwin and Heritage (1990), pre-sequences provide specific advantages both to their producer and to their recipients. First, pre-sequences enable parties to abort a projected interaction sequence in which conflict, disagreement, or rejection might emerge. Second, if the projected sequence is not aborted in this way, an affiliative outcome becomes more likely. In sum, pre-sequences are conversational devices through which dispreferred, face-threatening actions and sequences can be systematically avoided in interaction (Heritage 1984). In my German corpus, speakers orient to this preference relationship of offers over requests and commonly issue pre-requests. The cases presented in this chapter illustrate how speakers chose to issue a request, even though the pre-request expansion reveals contingencies on the request compliance. When the pre-request projects a disagreement or obstacle with granting the projected request, issuing a request may threaten or undermine the requester's relationship with his or her co-participant; in other words, by doing this, speakers put their co-participant under constraint to either agree to comply with the request or to reject it. This is the context in which the *wenn*-clause is produced. It seems that German speakers use the conditional *wenn*-clause (in such a context) as a device to display their affiliation with their co-participants by displaying their understanding of the circumstances and proposing to their recipient the preferred condition for their request compliance. Additional affiliation is achieved by incorporating into the *wenn*-clause elements of the co-particpant's prior turn. I propose that in combination with their sequential positioning, this specific design of the dispreferred request turns is supportive of "social solidarity" (Heritage 1984a). That is, co-participants follow patterns of behavior to interact with one another smoothly and to minimize the risk of confrontation.

Notes

1. For more information on compliment turns as pre-requests see Golato (2005).

2. Gohl (2000) suggests that the utterances introduced by the causal connector *weil* offer reasons for a previous utterance. The *weil*-clause in this example, however, seems to have a different function. This needs further research.

3. For a detailed description of "context ellipses" in everyday German conversation see Selting (1997).

4. The German word *auch* 'also' is pronounced here as *a* which is a form used in southern German regional dialects.

5. Günthner (1999b) notes that the subordinate *wenn*-clause may or may not be connected to the main clause by a resumptive element of "dann" (then) (9).

6. These were the most common turn-formats in my corpus. However, this does not mean that these are the only possible turn-formats (or composition) for pre-requests. There may well be other turn-formats that may serve as pre-requests.

CHAPTER 4

Accounts in request turns: Their placement and interactional function

4.1. Introduction

In this chapter, I continue exploring the relationship between the grammatical construction and interactional function of utterances by focusing on another design feature of request sequences. Specifically, the chapter offers an analysis of request sequences in which speakers provide their co-participants with an explanation or justification for their performed action (i.e., the request). I will offer a description of the internal organization of such account turn components in combination with their temporal placement and the action type they perform. The following segment (which has already been discussed in the previous chapter) illustrates an example of a request sequence in which the speaker provides an account. In the segment, Thomas asks his friend to find some pictures of him (Thomas) when he had long hair and to bring them along when he visits.

(1) Thomas/Mark (Fotos)

```
28      Thomas : .hhh wennst irgendwas findest   könnst     es   mitbringen
                 .hhh if you anything find+you could+you it   PRX+bring
                 .hhh if you find anything you could bring it along

29 ->   Thomas : weil    äh die eva die ä:h unterrichtet a   deutsch und
                 because uh the eva who u:h teaches         also german  and
                 because uh      eva who a:h also teaches german and studies

30 ->   Thomas : studiert hier und ha(h)t  irgendwie gmeint das   würd  sie
                 studies   here and ha(h)s somehow    said   that would she
                 here and kind of said that she would actually be

31 ->   Thomas : scho   interessieren.hhh
                 already interest.hhh
                 interested in.hhh

32      Markus : aha
                 uhu
                 uhu
```

```
33 -> Thomas : wie  ich  denn      so mit  langen haaren ausseh
                what i     actually so with long    hair    PRX+looked
                what i actually looked like with long hair

34 -> Markus: ja
              ja
              ja
```

In his multi-unit turn, Thomas performs two actions: he first expresses a request and then provides an account for it. In other words, he offers his recipient an explanation for his request (lines 30–31 and 33). Thomas' account is introduced by the causal connector *weil* 'because'.[1] An analysis of the request instances in the corpus suggests that request turns are frequently accompanied by some sort of an account for the performed request. In the following section, a general discussion of the interactional function of "accounts" in everyday conversations will be provided. This will be followed by a discussion of the composition and sequential placement of accounts for requests in everyday German conversation.

4.2. Accounts in everyday conversation

In general, "accounts" have been described as utterances through which speakers provide descriptions, explanations (justifications) and reasons for their inappropriate, unexpected or problematic actions (Antaki 1994; Cody and McLaughlin 1990; Draper 1988; Heritage 1984, 1988; Scott and Lyman 1968). Accounts in English discourse are regularly introduced by the conjunction *because* (or *'cause*) (Ford 1994: 536). As was noted in chapter one, particular turn types such as invitations, requests, and offers make certain next turns relevant or expectable, which are referred to as preferred or affiliative responses. Preferred responses are normally delivered rather directly and without any delays. A dispreferred response, on the other hand, is typically delivered with some delays, hesitations, and an account for not providing the preferred response (Pomerantz 1984). For example, Heritage (1984a) notes that social activities such as offers, invitations and requests generally project acceptance as their next turn or response, and that a failure to response to any of these activities affirmatively is "accountable" (p. 270). Thus accounts typically occur when speakers perform an action which has the potential of being interpreted by their co-participant as unexpected or disaffiliative. Their job is, then, to perform some kind of "remedial work", i.e., to change the meaning of an act that might be understood by its recipient as offensive into what can be understood as acceptable (Goffman 1971: 109). In other words, when speakers perform an unexpected, dispreferred or disaffiliative action, they frequently engage in this "remedial" action by offering some kind of explanation for their situationally disaffiliative action so that their co-participant will not think unfavorably of them (Heritage 1984a; Cody and McLaughlin 1990). Therefore, accounts have been described as actions in which speakers engage to avoid friction in social interaction and thereby maintain social solidarity (Heritage 1984a). Heritage (1984a) notes that accounts which occur in such interactional environments, i.e., as part of dispreferred responses, generally indicate a lack of ability rather than an unwillingness to perform the preferred response (for example, accepting an invitation). He also notes that because of their "no fault" ability form, these kinds of accounts do not threaten the "face" of either party or the relationship between them. Thus, accounts which are designed in these ways function as "threat- and conflict-avoidance" procedures, and serve to maintain social solidarity (p. 273).

Accounts may not only be a required design feature of disaffiliative second actions to invitations, requests and offers: they are also found in disaffilative/dispreferred first actions. For example, Antaki (1994) and Schegloff (1995) have shown that accounts may be observed in dispreferred first parts, such as request turns. In such instances, production of the dispreferred action may be accompanied by features such as mitigations, accounts, and "excuses" for the recipient. Schegloff (in press) suggests that all of these features may occur within the request turn and thus defer the production of the request (p. 81–83). Antaki (1994) notes that when speakers perform a request that is interactionally unexpected, they frequently provide an account, i.e., some kind of explanation for their unexpected action (p. 87).[2] Similar to accounts in dispreferred responses, accounts in disaffiliative first actions serve to avoid any potential social conflict. This interactional function of accounts can also be found in other languages. In the following section, I will explore instances of accounts in request sequences in German conversation and analyze their composition and temporal placement. Furthermore, I will discuss how the content, placement, and even syntactic structure of accounts within the request sequence may be related to preference organization.

4.3. Accounts in German request sequences

An investigation of the German request sequences in my corpus reveals that the majority of request turns are multi-unit turns consisting of two or more components, such as a request, an account, and some other talk. Similar to English speakers, Germans frequently provide an explanation when making a request. As was noted above, studies in English suggest that accounts in request turns may occur before the request and therefore defer the production of this dispreferred action (Schegloff in press). In my conversational corpus, however, the majority of instances of accounts which are expressed in causal clauses occur only after the request action that they account for.[3] Of the 30 request sequences, speakers provide accounts for their requests in 60% of them. In 28% of the request sequences the account is built in the request turn, while in 28% of them the account occurs after the request has been granted. An account may also occur after a speaker projects a rejection of the request to be granted (22%). Furthermore, the account is introduced by the coordinating conjunction *denn* 'because' in only two request sequences. Nor can it be said that all accounts are marked by a causal connector, since in only 16% of the instances was an account offered without being prefaced by a causal connector.

In the present chapter I describe the abovementioned categories of request plus account instances in everyday German. The analysis focuses on three design features of account utterances in request turns: (a) their temporal placement within the request turn; (b) their grammatical structure; and (c) their content. Through this examination, I show that not only the content and placement within the request turn and within the sequence, but also the grammatical structure of account instances may be interpreted as part of the mitigation strategy which is supportive of social solidarity.

4.3.1   Accounts built into request turns

In this section, I describe request turn types in which speakers place an account component immediately following their request. Segment 1 (repeated here) exemplifies such an instance. Again, this is an excerpt in which Thomas makes a request even though his pre-request and its expanded talk displayed some problems and contingencies with granting his request (illustrated in chapter 3). Thomas requests that his friend bring some pictures of him (Thomas) with long hair, upon the condition that his friend finds those pictures (line 28). Note that following his request, Thomas provides an explanation for his request (lines 28, 29, 30, and 33).

(1)   Thomas/Mark (Fotos)

```
28 ->   Thomas: .hhh  wennst irgendwas findest   könnst    es mitbringen
                 .hhh  if you  anything find+you  could+you it PRX+bring
                 .hhh if you find anything you could bring it along

29 ->   Thomas : weil    äh  die eva die ä:h unterrichtet a    deutsch und
                  because uh  the eva who u:h teaches        also german and
                  because uh eva who a:h also teaches german and studies

30 ->   Thomas : studiert hier und ha(h)t irgendwie gmeint das würd sie
                  studies here and ha(h)s somehow said that would she
                  here and kind of said that she would actually be
```

```
31 ->   Thomas  : scho      interessieren.hhh
                  already   interest.hhh
                  interested in.hhh

32      Markus  : aha
                  uhu
                  uhu

33 ->   Thomas  : wie ich denn       so  mit  langen haaren ausseh
                  what i    actually  so  with long   hair   PRX+looked
                  what i actually looked like with long hair

34 ->   Markus  : ja
                  ja
                  ja
```

Thomas expresses the reason for his request in a clause which is marked by the causal connector *weil*, a conjunction that is regularly used to introduce causal clauses in German (Duden 1998; Engel 1991). The deployment of the causal connector *weil* in Thomas' request turn conveys some relation between what the speaker has just said and what he is about to say. Another important feature of Thomas' account component is the placement of the *weil*-clause. As we can see, Thomas' account component is placed directly adjacent to his request clause, thereby expanding the request turn. Note also that the connector *weil* is produced at a position that is a possible completion of the turn (Sacks et al. 1974). According to Schegloff (1982), speakers may employ conversational devices in order to "rush through" their talk and to keep the floor. Examples of such conversational devices include increasing the speed of one's talk at a possible completion point, or formulating one's talk in such a manner as to project continuous talk. Thomas' request turn is a multi-unit turn in which the first TCU is syntactically complete at *wennst irgendwas findest könnst es mitbringen* 'if you find anything could you bring it along'. His turn is also "pragmatically" complete (Ford and Thompson 1996)[4] since it recognizably implements an action (a request); Thomas, however, moves to extend the talk in his turn by adding a causal *weil*-clause. By using the causal connector *weil*, Thomas not only signals to his co-participant that his turn in not completed, but also that a specific type of unit, i.e., a causal clause, will follow shortly. Thus, Thomas' post-positioned account expresses a justification for his contingent request.

Ford (1993) notes that in American English, there are frequently pauses and disfluencies either before or after the conjunction when adverbial clauses (including causal clauses) occur in post-position (p. 91). In this data segment, there is a speech perturbation in the form of some hesitation immediately following the production of the causal connector *weil*. It seems that by producing the causal connector *weil*, Thomas secures multiple units of talk which may contain the reason for his request. Following the speech perturbation, Thomas utters a female's name (a friend/colleague) and the relative pronoun *die* 'who' (line 29) before producing another speech perturbation. Note that after mentioning *Eva* (the friend/colleague's name), Thomas inserts some information about her (she also teaches German and studies at Thomas' university). In doing so, Thomas provides his co-participant with some background information about the person who will benefit from Thomas' request, thus making his request understandable and possibly acceptable. Following this, he produces the core motive for his request, namely that his friend is interested in seeing pictures of him with long hair (lines 30, 31, and 33). Heritage (1984a) notes that accounts for dispreferred responses to invitations or offers generally have a form of "no fault" quality, since they indicate an inability rather than an unwillingness to accept an invitation, offer, etc. Additionally, Heritage suggests that accounts with "no fault" quality do not threaten the "face" of either party or the relationship between them. Thus, accounts which are designed this way function as threat- and conflict-avoidance procedures, and serve to maintain social solidarity (p. 273). It appears that Thomas' account has a similar "no fault" design. That is, by explaining that a third party (i.e., Eva) wishes to see those pictures to which he has no access, he indicates that the motive for his request is not himself but another person (a friend) and a matter over which he has no control.

Note that Thomas' account is produced following his contingent request (recall that there were some hesitant responsive actions to Thomas' pre-request). I argue that the request turn in this data segment is designed in such a way as to pursue a preferred response (here, granting the request) from the co-participant. In other words, by introducing some background information and a "no fault" explanation for his request, Thomas provides information for his co-participant to understand the situation and the reason for his request. In so doing, Thomas makes his request more acceptable to his co-participant. Furthermore, by placing the background information and the account immediately after the request utterance, Thomas secures the delivery of these two components before his co-participant's response to his request.

The next excerpt (segment 2) provides a similar instance of a request turn in which an account for the request is placed immediately after the request utterance. This excerpt is taken from a conversation between Dora and her mother (Mutti) in Germany. After a brief conversation about the family cat and how it has been gaining weight (not included in the transcript), Dora performs a request (lines 2–3): she asks her mother if she is able to tell their mutual friend, Miriam, that Dora has a certain set of pictures. Following her request, Dora provides an explanation for it, namely that their friend, Miriam, wants to see some of those pictures (line 4).

(2)   Dora/Mutti (Fotos)

```
01      Mutti: .hh ha dieses viech
                .hh ha this    animal
                .hh ha this    animal

02 ->   Dora : mh °naja° äh he .hh hum. ah kannst   vielleicht der mi-na
                mh °well° uh he .hh hum. oh can+you maybe       the mi-no
                mh °well° uh he .hh hum. oh can you maybe       the mi-no

03 ->   Dora : ich schreib jetzt ihr selber mal der Miriam mal sagen dass
                i    write   now to her myself PT  the Miriam MP  say    that
                i'll write her myself just tell Miriam that i have

04 ->   Dora : ich fotos    hab weil   die will a     eweng was sehen.
                i   pictures have because she wants also a bit some see.
                pictures because she also wants to see some of them.

05          (0.8)

06      Mutti: auch die: photos    von mir,?
                also the: pictures from me,?
                my pictures, too?

07      Dora : ha       ha
                yeah    yeah
                yeah    yeah

08          (0.5)

09      Dora : ha=
                ha=
                ha=

10      Mutti: =ich muss sowieso's mal die woch nunter ins
                =i   must anyway    MP  this week down   to
                =i   have to go this week anyway down to

11      Mutti: theater eingladen,
                theater invited,
                invited to the theater,

12      Dora : mh mh
                mh mh
                mh mh

13      Mutti: weil   wir mal wieder ins    theater genga,
                because we MP again  to the theater go,
                because we're going to the theater again,

14      Dora : ha ha,
                mh mh,
                mh mh
```

```
15          (.)

16    Dora : ach [da      kannste
           oh  [there  can+you
           oh  [there  you can
              [
17    Mutti: [un  da     nimm ich se     mal mit.
           [and there take i    them MP with.
           [and i'll   take them with me.

18    Dora : ha oh ja   ha kannste noch machen.  .hh ha[ha
           mh oh yes   mh can+you still do.     .hh mh[mh
           mh oh yeah  mh you can do that too.   . mh[mh
```

Dora provides an account *weil die will a eweng was sehen* 'because she also wants to see some of them' immediately after her request. Similar to the previous excerpt, the account is expressed in a causal clause which is marked by the causal connector *weil*. Also note that the causal *weil*-clause is placed at a position that is a possible completion of the turn. Dora's request utterance *der Miriam mal sagen dass ich fotos hab* 'tell Miriam that I have pictures' is syntactically and pragmatically complete. Furthermore, both clauses are produced in one intonation contour, thus there is no discontinuity between the clauses. In doing so, Dora secures a multi-unit turn and provides the account as a continuation of the request turn. Dora explains to her mother that their friend, Miriam, wishes to see the pictures. Similar to the account turn in the previous data segment, Dora's account has a "no fault" quality, i.e., the request is made for the benefit of a third party- a situation which is out of Dora's control. Furthermore, Dora's account is produced before her mother has responded to the request. By providing an explanation for her request, Dora pursues a preferred response to her request. Note that Dora's mother offers to take the pictures to town with her (line 17). She not only agrees to tell their friend about the pictures, but also offers to take to her the ones she has.

Thus far I have discussed that similar to English conversations, accounts in German are a design feature of requests. The data fragments exemplified how account components are marked by the causal connector *weil* and that they may be placed immediately following the request utterance. The analysis also showed that the *weil*-clauses may be intonationally connected with the reprevious material and thereby may be built in the request turn as a continuation of the turn immediately after the TCU of request is pragmatically complete. By placing their account clause right after the request TCU, speakers secure the opportunity to provide their justification for their request. I also discussed how speakers provide an account for their request by reference to "no fault" for their request: the requests are for the benefit of a third party, and the speakers have no access to the object (segment 1) or the person to whom information must be delivered (segment 2). I also stated that by providing some background information and reason for their request, speakers make their requests more acceptable to their co-participant before they respond to it.

However, not all accounts in my corpus are placed immediately after the request utterance. In the next subsection, I illustrate how speakers provide an account for a request after a possible dispreferred response is projected.

4.3.2   Accounts following a projected dispreferred response

Another placement for accounts is a context in which a response to the request is rather hesitant and in which possible disagreement with the request is projectable. The next excerpt, segment 3, exemplifies such an instance. This is a phone conversation recorded in Germany between Tina, a student who lives in a university town, and her mother. Tina is having a hard time finding a document on her computer and therefore believes that it could be on their family computer at home. She calls home and asks her mother to look for her document. In lines 7 and 8, she provides an explanation for her request.

```
(3)   Tina/Mutti (Dokument)

01    Tina : kling   gut.
             sounds  good.
             sounds  good.
02           (.)

03    Tina : .hhh a:h ah mensch pass   mal auf wenn's    mal
             .hhh o:h oh man      watch MP PRX when you  MP
             .hhh o:h oh man listen the next time you get

04    Tina : wieder anen    computer gehst. [mh?
             again  to the computer go.     [mh?
             to the computer.              [mh?
                                           [
05    Mutti:                               [mhm,
                                           [mhm,
                                           [mhm,

06    Tina : suchauftrag.
             searching task.
             searching task.

07           (0.5)

08    Mutti: mh,
             mh,
             mh,
09 -> Tina : .hhh weil   ich hab  gedacht ich hätt's die ganz  zeit
             .hhh because i   have thought i   had it the whole time
             .hhh because i thought that i had it the whole time
```

```
10 ->  Tina :  mit-hab    ich aber irgendwie net. .hhh ich hab   doch letztes
                with-have  i   but  somehow   not. .hh  I    have MP    last
                with me-but somehow i  don't. .hhh i  have actually last

11     Tina :  jahr ….
                year…
                year.
```

Tina's request refers to a searching task (line 4), which after a pause of (0.5) receives a minimal response of *mh,*. Silences occurring immediately after a request may be heard by speakers as possible rejection (Davidson 1984). Thus, the subsequent pause and the minimal response to Tina's request display some possible hesitation or problem with the request. Note also that Tina's request TCU consist of a "compound turn-constructional unit" (Lerner 1991), which is constructed by a *wenn*-clause and the request utterance. As was noted in chapter 3, speakers frequently position a conditional *wenn*-clause before their request utterance. The initial position of the conditional *wenn*-clause and its content allow the recipient to infer the projection of a request, i.e., Tina's initial placement of a conditional *wenn*-clause (lines 1–2) can be heard to project an upcoming request. Following her "response pursuit" marker (Harren 2001; Jefferson 1980) in line 2 and her mother's recipient token *mhm* in line 3, Tina utters her request *suchauftrag* 'searching task'. After a pause of 0.5 second, Tina's mother responds to her request minimally (line 6). It is in this context that Tina offers her mother an explanation and justification for her request. Note that Tina's request is very generic – she has not mentioned yet what exactly she is looking for. This may be an explanation for the pause following her request. Tina's account, expressed in a *weil*-clause, explains that she first thought she had a certain (as-of-yet-unspecified) document with her the whole time but somehow doesn't (lines 7–8). Note that in her account utterance, Tina is not only justifying her request but also at the same time explaining what she needs on their computer, namely a document. It could be argued that the document is not mentioned in her request turn since one can infer from the context, i.e., computer and searching task, that what is being talked about is searching for a document. Similar to the previous account for request examples, Tina's account indicates inability to access the requested object. It seems that by providing a justification for her action, Tina is pursuing an acceptance from her mother to grant her request.

This subsection illustrated that accounts in request sequences may result from interaction between co-participants. That is, speakers provide an explanation for their request when their request turn fails to engender a preferred responsive action from their co-participant. Such accounts may be introduced with a causal *weil*-clause and may pursue a preferred response from their recipient.

Accounts for requests may also occur after a request has been granted by the co-participant; this will be discussed in the following subsection.

4.3.3   Accounts subsequent to request acceptance

Speakers may provide an explanation for their request after their co-participant agrees to comply with the request. The following data fragment (segment 4) exemplifies such an instance. This data fragment was taken from a conversation between two sisters, Dora and Carla. Dora is a German student in an exchange program in the US who calls her sister in Germany. This call is placed shortly before Dora will visit her family during the coming Christmas.

(4)   Dora/Carla (Schlittschuh)

```
01      Dora : he. he. o::h gott skifahren wäre  was   me machen
                he. he. o::h god  skiing     would what  we make
                he. He. o::h god skiing would be something we

02      Dora : [können.
                [could.
                [could do.
                [
03      Carla: [.hhh horch mal ä:h he:: .hh genau    da     kann ich dich
                [.hhh listen MP u:h he:: .hh exactly there  can  i   you
                [.hhh listen u:h he:: .hh exactly now i can

04      Carla: mal gleich anbaggern brauchst du ä:hm, im
                MP  now       bug           need     you u:hm, in
                bug you now do you uh:m, need your ice skates

05      Carla: wintersemester   wenn du   wieder nüberfliegst deine
                winter semester when you again   PRX+fly       your
                in the winter semester when you fly over

06      Carla: schlittschuh?
                ice skates?
                again?

07          (0.8)

08      Dora : ä:hm, pfr: .hh kaum    ä:h   ne. .hh ä:-ä:[in law-1-
                u:hm, pfr: .hh hardly u:h   no. .hh u:-u:[in law-1-
                u:hm, pfr: .hh hardly u:h no. .hh u:-u: [in law-1-
                                                         [
09      Carla:                                           [gut.
                                                         [good.
                                                         [good.
```

```
10    Dora : lawrence da    gib's    keine schlittschubahn also
             lawrence there give'it no   ice-skating ring so
             Lawrence there aren't any ice-skating rings so

11    Carla: gut  wunderbar weil   dann nehm ich die   mit [( )
             good wonderful because then take i   them with[( )
             good wonderful because then i'll take them      [( )
                                                             [
12    Dora :                                               [ne
                                                          [no
                                                          [no

13    Dora : kannst  ( ) kannsch-kannst  mit  nehmen kannste mal
             can+you ( ) can+you-can+you with take  can+you MP
             you can ( ) you      can-you can  take them you can

14    Dora : schleifen lassen wennst wi(h)llst   he hehehe
             sand      leave  if+you wa(h)nt+you he hehehe
             have them sanded if you wa(h)nt he hehehe

15    Dora : he .hhh [he
             he .hhh [he
             he .hhh [he
                     [
16    Carla: [ja   genau,  zum beispiel ne   ich überlege
             [yes  exactly, for example  right i   think
             [yes exactly, for example right i'll think about

17 -> Carla : weil   i weiss ned selbe wo   diese dinge  sind
             because i know   not self where these things are
             it because i don't know myself where they are
```

In line 17, Carla provides an account for her request of borrowing her sister's skates (for detailed analysis of this request sequence, see segment 1 in chapter 3). Carla's account occurs after her sister accepts her request (line 13). Following her offer, Dora also suggest to her sister to have the skates sanded. After responding to Dora's suggestion (line 16), Carla continues her turn by offering a reason for her request: she explains that she does not know where she put her skates (line 17). Similar to the previous examples of accounts for request, Carla's account refers to the lack of access to the object which she is requesting. Note also that her account is introduced by the causal connector *weil* and that it is placed after her co-participant grants her request (a preferred response). Recall that in the previous data segments, accounts occurred before the recipient responded to the request or at a position in which a dispreferred response was projectable. It was argued that one interactional job performed by accounts in this sequential placement is to make their requests more acceptable. In this excerpt, however, the account occurs after the request has already been accepted. It seems that accounts in such situations more typically address the dispreferred action of requests. As was mentioned earlier, accounts perform some kind of "remedial work" (Goffman 1971) when speakers perform a dispreferred or disaffiliative action. It seems that when speakers do perform dispreferred actions such as requests, the next logical conversational move is to offer some sort of explanation or justification for their dispreferred action so that their co-participant will not think unfavorably of them. I argue that accounts which occur after the recipient has accepted to comply with the request, i.e., the "after-request-acceptance" position, perform "remedial work". In other words, it appears that their focus is on repairing the damage the dispreferred action may have caused to the recipient's face. On the other hand, accounts which occur before the recipient's acceptance to comply with the request, i.e., in the "before-request-response" position, appear to perform different interactional work. I argue that because of their sequential placement, they focus on pursuing an acceptance for response from their recipient.

Let us examine another instance of an account placed after the request has received a preferred responsive action. The next excerpt (segment 5) is taken from a conversation between Markus, who is in a student exchange program in the United States, and his friend, Klaus, in Germany. Klaus asks his friend if he could get him some information about the price of a specific tennis racket, since that particular brand is quite expensive in Germany (lines 2–5, 8–9, and 36–37).

(5)   Markus/Klaus (Tennisschläger)

```
01     Markus : ich glaube   [das
                i   believe  [that
                i   believe  [it
                             [
02     Klaus  : [MARKUS genau   das   wollte ich
                [MARKUS exactly that wanted  i
                [MARKUS exactly that's what  i

03     Klaus  : noch  bitten
                still ask
                wanted to ask you

04            (0.2)

05     Klaus  : erkundige dich     ma:l  nach 'em tennisschläger.
                inform    yourself MP    after a  tennis racket.
                get some information about a tennis racket.

06            (0.5)

07     Markus : ja=
                yes=
                yes=
```

```
08    Klaus   : =und  zwar  (0.2) nach   einem wilson prostar
               =and  MP    (0.2) after  a     Wilson prostar
               =about      (0.2) a           wilson prostar


09    Klaus   : der edberg schläger.
                The edberg racket.
                the edberg racket.


10    Markus  : also  ein moment ich muss mal  aufschreiben da.
                so    a   moment i   must MP PRX+write      there.
                just a moment there i have to make a note


11            (0.5)


12    Markus  : .hh also?
                .hh so?
                .hh so?


13    Klaus   : wilson.
                wilson.
                wilson.


14      (.)


15    Klaus   : ne?
                right?
                right?


16            (0.2)


17    Markus  : ja,?
                yes,?
                yea,?


18    Klaus   : und der heisst   prostar
                and the name+it prostar
                and it's called prostar


19            (1.2)


20    Markus  : pro-
                pro-
                pro-


21            (0.2)


22    Klaus   : st [ar
                st [ar
                st [ar
                   [
23    Markus  :    [plural. ja?
                   [plural. yea?
                   [plural. right?
```

```
24                 (0.5)

25      Klaus   : bitte?
                  please?
                  pardon?

26      Markus  : plural? stars? p- mit s?
                  plural? stars? p-with s?
                  plural? stars? p-with s?

27                 (0.5)

28      Klaus   : star
                  star
                  star

29                 (.)

30      Klaus   : [prostar
                  [prostar
                  [prostar
                  [
31      Markus  : [ja
                  [yes
                  [yea

32      Markus  : ja.
                  yes.
                  yea.

33      Klaus   : nicht stars sondern star eigentlich
                  not    stars but      star actually
                  not stars but  star   actually

34      Markus  : mhm
                  mhm
                  mhm

35      Klaus   : aber das   ist der der edberg schläger, .hhh
                  but  that is   the the edberg racket,    .hhh
                  but  that's the the edberg racket, .hhh

36      Klaus   : (.) w-we-erk-kundige dich    mal wieviel  der  da
                  (.) w-we-in-form      yourself MP how much the  there
                  (.) w-we-find out how much it costs

37      Klaus   : kostet  und schreib mir das mal.
                  cost+it and write   me   it  MP
                  there       and write me

38      (0.8)

39      Markus  : ja   okay
                  yes okay
                  yea okay
```

```
40 -> Klaus  : un   dann kann  ich  d-dir  vielleicht schicken  weil
                and  then can   i    y-you  maybe      send     because
                and  then i can maybe send y-you because

41 -> Klaus  : ich   hab hier jetzt da  ein vom   (  )  der kostet
                i      have now there    one from (  )   it  costs
                i have one here from the (  )it costs

42 -> Klaus  : hier  fast    fünfhundert  mark.  .hhh
                here  almost  five hundred marks..hhh
                here  almost  five hundred marks..hhh

43    Markus : ja
                yes
                yea

44    Klaus  : [und- der
                [and-the
                [and-it
                [
45    Markus:  [und du    brauchst  ( ) also wilson ist grade   die
                [and you   need+you  ( ) MP   wilson is  exactly the
                [and you   need      ( ) MP   Wilson is  the     exact

46    Markus:  marke die  ja  in ist. [ne,
                brand the  yes in is.  [right,
                brand that's   in.     [right,
```

In lines 2–5, and 8–9, Klaus asks his friend to get some information about a specific tennis racket (a Wilson Prostar). After some repair and clarification on the name of the model, Klaus repeats his request (lines 36–37). This time his request is more specific: he asks his friend to find out about the price of such a tennis racket in the United States. Following Klaus' request and a pause (0.8) Markus agrees to grant his friend's request (line 39). Note that in line 40, Klaus comments that he could then maybe send his friend money. Note also that Klaus does not utter the word money, but from the context it can be inferred that he is referring to money. Following this, he provides his friend with an explanation for his request, namely that that model is quite expensive in Germany (it costs almost 500 Marks). Again, the account for the request in this data fragment is expressed in a causal *weil*-clause. Furthermore, Klaus' account refers to the high price of the racket – a matter that is clearly not his fault. Similar to the previous instances of accounts for requests, the speaker requests a service which the co-participant can perform since he or she shas access to the object or person (in the case of segment 2) while the speaker (i.e., the requester) does not.

This excerpt illustrates that speakers may provide an account for their request even after it has received a preferred response. Looking at this request sequence, we can note that Klaus actually performs three requests: (a) he first asks his friend to get some information about a tennis racket (lines 2–5); (b) he then asks his friend to find out how much a Wilson tennis racket costs and to send this information to him (36 and 37); and finally, (c) he implicitly asks his friend to purchase the racket in the United States (39–41). I argue that the last request has been made implicitly and that from the context of the previous request (finding out about the price and offering to send money), it can be inferred that Klaus wants his friend to purchase the racket in the Unites States. Furthermore, I argue that Klaus' requests are connected to one another in the sense that the first request leads to the second request, and that the second request leads to the third request. Note that Klaus' requests receive preferred responsive actions: Markus agrees to comply with his friend's first request in line 10, and with his second request in line 36. Following Markus' acceptance to comply with the request, Klaus performs a third request, which is formulated implicitly. It is at this position that Klaus provides an explanation for his request. I argue that Klaus' account not only addresses the last request, but also the previous two requests. In particular, I argue that Klaus' account can be interpreted as being produced in a before-request response position with the interactional job of making his last request more acceptable. Klaus' account can also be described as being produced in an after-request-acceptance position, since it is placed after his first two requests' preferred responses. In other words, it seems that the account in this segment is also addressing the action(s) that have already been produced (i.e., the previous requests).

In this subsection, I examined instances in which speakers provide an account for their request after their request has received a preferred response, that is, an acceptance to comply with the request. Similar to the previous examples of accounts in request sequences, the account turns discussed in this section are expressed in causal *weil*-clauses. I also discussed the different sequential placement of the account turns and what their specific placement interactionally achieves. I argued that accounts that are placed in the before-request-response position pursue a preferred responsive action from the co-participant. It appears that accounts that are produced in the after-request-acceptance position may be understood as remedial work which addresses the co-participant's face. In other words, such post request placement of accounts functions as "threat-and conflict avoidance" (Heritage 1984a) strategy.

In the next section, I examine the grammatical structure of instances of accounts for requests and their relationship to preference organization.

4.4. Accounts for requests: Their grammatical structure

In the above sections we saw that accounts for requests in German conversation are commonly marked by the causal connector *weil*. In this section, I will examine the grammatical structure, specifically the word order, of such instances of accounts for request which are expressed in a causal *weil*-clause. Looking at the grammatical structure of such *weil*-clauses in my corpus, I find that they all display main-clause word order, i.e., finite verb in the second position. This specific structure of *weil*-clauses is considered to be ungrammatical by standard reference grammars, though it has been observed in spoken discourse and in specific contexts (Günthner 1993, 1996; Keller 1995; Küper 1984, 1991; Scheutz 2001; Uhmann 1998; Wegener 1993).

In general, there are two different word orders in German: (a) main clause word order, which requires the verb-second position: for example, in the sentence *ich frage meinen Vater* 'I ask my father', the conjugated verb *frage* is in the second position; and (b) verb-final position, which is the standard word order for subordinate (dependent) clause constructions. A subordinate or dependent clause is a type of clause which is introduced by a subordinate conjunction such as *weil* 'because', *dass* 'that', *ob* 'if', *wenn* 'if', etc. An example of unmarked word order for subordinate clause constructions would be *Ich frage meinen Vater, weil er die Antwort weiss* 'I ask my father, because he knows the answer'. The conjugated verb *weiss* is placed in the final position of the subordinate *weil*-clause.

Research on German discourse suggests that speakers are increasingly tending to use main clause word order, i.e., verb-second position, in *weil*-clauses, which is considered incorrect by many prescriptive grammar reference books; and that the choice between the two patterns is systematically determined by semantic and discourse-pragmatic principles. However, it is worth mentioning that only a few of these studies have actually examined the occurrences of *weil*-clauses with finite verb in the second position in naturally occurring conversation. I will provide here a summary of the findings of these studies that have used spontaneous conversation as their corpus.

In her investigation of verb-second causal *weil*-clauses in everyday German conversation, Günthner (1993, 1996) suggests that there are semantic differences between the two variations of word order for *weil*-clauses. According to Günthner, tthe verb-second *weil*-clause is used to express epistemic causality, i.e., the causal *weil*-clause does not express a factual reason but something more on the epistemic level, whereas the verb-final *weil*-clause is deployed for propositional causality, i.e., such causal *weil*-clause provide an account for the state of affairs that is referred to in the main clause.[5] A discussion of the two *weil*-clauses at the syntactic level suggests that they are two distinct entities: verb-second clauses are no longer dependent clauses and thus can only be postpositioned; that is, they can only be placed after the main clause. On the other hand, verb-final *weil*-clauses are subordinate adverbial clauses and can therefore be moved to the preverbal position of the main clause (*Vorfeld*) (Pasch 1997; Uhmann 1998). The prosodic properties of the two different *weil*-clauses in German conversation have also been addressed by these researchers. In particular, they propose a correlation between the prosodic properties of *weil*-clauses and their syntactic structure, in that there is a cohesive intonation contour over both the main-clause and the verb-final *weil*-clause. The fact that they are prosodically produced as one unit suggests that the verb-final *weil*-clause is syntactically integrated into the main clause. By contrast, the verb-second *weil*-clause and its main-clause are each prosodically produced as two separate units (the main clause of such *weil*-clauses is produced with final falling intonation). Furthermore, these studies have shown that there is usually a brief pause between the conjunction *weil* and the rest of the phrase in the verb-second *weil*-clause. These findings suggest that the verb-second *weil*-clause is not syntactically integrated into the main-clause (Güntner 1993, 1996; Pasch 1997). Scheutz (2001) examines verb-second *weil*-clauses in multi-turn sequences of talk and notes that verb-final *weil*-clauses are frequently used as cohesive devices for turns in conversations since they are syntactically dependent. In other words, speakers use the dependent verb-final *weil*-clause to make a connection to an utterance produced in previous turns. On a more pragmatic level, it has been proposed that *weil*-clauses with main-clause word order function as an independent clause and therefore carry their own illocutionary force (Günthner 1993, 1996; Pasch 1997; Scheutz, 2001; Uhmann 1998). For example, in her German conversational corpus, Günthner (1993, 1996) notes particular interactional environments in which verb-second causal *weil*-clauses occur. One interactional environment in which such clauses occur is when a preferred/relevant recipient response does not follow, or when a dispreferred response is projected. For example:

(Günthner 1996: 327)

	22	Udo:	*ihr habt nicht s-(.) zufällig s'Blasrohr, (-) oder?*
	23	Maria:	*°he eh.°*
=>24		Udo:	*weil da is ja em Peter sein Flugartikel drin. (-) über? (-)*

	22	Udo:	you don't happen to have the Blasrohr here (-) do you
	23	Maria:	°no°
=> 24		Udo:	because Peter's article on flying is in it (-) about (-)

Udo makes a pre-request (line 22), a question checking whether some preconditions exist for the action to be performed; Maria's declination indicates that the precondition for action is not fulflled (line 23). Following this, Udo gives an explanation for his pre-request and withholds an explicit request. Günthner suggests (1996) that a *weil*-clause with main-clause word order becomes an independent clause, and that therefore each type of clause practices a different illocutionary force.[6] Another context in which main clause word order *weil*-clauses occur is when the *weil*-clause provides the cause for the preceding action, for example, when speakers provide an account for their request:

(Günthner 1993: 41)

24S: *hol-hol mir bitte die Kanne da runter.-*
25   *weil-ich kann grad nicht aufstehen.*

24S: bring-bring me please the pot over there.-
25   because-i cannot get up now.

Günthner proposes that the two clauses, the request in line 24 and the causal *weil*-clause in line 25, are two independent utterances (note that the *weil*-clause displays main clause word order) and they therefore each carry their own illocutionary force (p. 41). Furthermore, she suggests that this proposition is also supported by prosodic means in that these two clauses, request and account, carry their own intonation contours. As a matter of fact, she notes that with such exchanges, there are often some prosodic discontinuities such as pauses or differences in tempo and volume between the two clauses. Günthner does not discuss, however, whether this is the only sequential placement (i.e., immediately following the request turn) for causal *weil*-clauses with marked word order.

As I noted earlier, all of the causal *weil*-clauses in my collection of instances of accounts for requests display the marked word order, in which the finite verb appears in the second position. This supports Günthner's findings of verb-second causal *weil*-clauses following a request turn. My analysis, however, suggests two additional placements for verb-second *weil*-clauses in request sequences: after certain projected dispreferred responses, and after the recipient has already responded to the request. In the following section, I will provide a detailed analysis of the grammatical structure of causal *weil*-clauses and their sequential placement in my collection of request sequences. From these analyses, I will argue that the particular grammatical structure of verb-second *weil*-clauses may be understood as a feature of the preference organization of request sequences.

When considering the accounts for requests exemplified in the segments below, we find that the accounts are marked by the causal connector *weil*, which indicates that what follows is an explanation for the previous action. A feature that the majority of the discussed examples share is that the account turns are composed of multiple clauses, which results in the turns being relatively long. Let us now revisit the account turns illustrated in this chapter and take a closer look at their grammatical structure, in particular the position of the finite verb, and the interactional work that they perform.

(1)   Thomas/Mark (Fotos)

```
29 ->  Thomas : weil    äh die eva die ä:h unterrichtet a    deutsch und
                 because uh the eva who u:h teaches       also german  and
                 because uh eva who a:h also teaches german and studies

30 ->  Thomas : studiert hier und ha(h)t  irgendwie gmeint  das  würd  sie
                 studies  here and ha(h)s  somehow   said    that would she
                 here and kind of said that she would actually be

31 ->  Thomas: scho    interessieren.hhh
                already interest.hhh
                interested in.hhh

32     Markus: aha
               uhu
               uhu

33 ->  Thomas : wie  ich denn      so mit  langen haaren ausseh
                 what i   actually so with long   hair   PRX+looked
                 what i   actually looked like with long hair

34 ->  Markus: ja
               ja
               ja
```

In segment 1, the account turn is initiated with the causal connector *weil*, marking the turn as an account. As was discussed above, accounts for requests may refer to a "lack of access" to the requested object. In segment 1, Thomas does not have access to the pictures which have been requested from him by a third party. Thomas' multi-clausal account turn is composed of four clauses:

```
(a)  die eva die ä:h unterrichtet a deutsch
(b)  und studiert hier
(c)  und ha(h)t irgendwie gmeint
(d)  das würd sie scho interessieren
(e)  wie ich mit langen Haaren ausseh
```

The core account or justification for Thomas' request is: *weil äh die eva hat irgendwie gmeint das würd sie scho interessieren* 'because uh Eva kind of thought that she would be interested in seeing them'. Notice that the speaker inserts some talk, in this case background information about the friend who would benefit from the request, between the causal connector *weil* and the projectable causal clause, which expresses the actual justification for the request. The causal clause in this instance is a compound TCU (Lerner 1991), *die eva hat irgendwie gmeint* 'Eva kind of thought' + *das würd sie scho interessieren* 'that she would be interested in them'. It appears that the insertion of a "parenthetical remark" (Lerner 2004) into an otherwise projectable TCU delays the occurrence of the core components of the account (*hat irgendwie gmeint das würde sie scho interessieren*). Note also that the causal clause to which the causal connector *weil* refers displays main clause word order. As was noted earlier, the word order structure of German differs from English in that in specific sentence/clause types (such as in subordinate clauses) the finite verb is placed in the final position of the clause. Therefore, in subordinate clauses with finite verb in the final position the semantic expression or upshot of what is being said may be unspecified until the verb appears at the end of the clause.[7] Notice that in the above data segment, the speaker places the finite verb in second position in the causal *weil*-clause, thereby accelerating the occurrence of the finite verb which carries the essential semantic meaning of the causal clause. I argue that positioning the finite verb in the second position appears to address two interactional issues which may have to do with facilitating co-participants' understanding of the multi-unit account turns. First, the early (second) positioning of the finite verb seems to cognitively facilitate the understanding of multi-unit account turns. In other words, by positioning the finite verb in the second position, Thomas allows his co-participant, Mark, to project aspects of his account turn. The finite verb in the causal clause is the auxiliary verb *hat* 'has', which not only carries the information of time (something that Eva did in the past) but also allows speakers to project the trajectory of the following talk. Additionally, an early positioning of the finite verb in such a multi-unit account turn may also function as a cohesive device which facilitates understanding of the account turn. Recall that Thomas begins his account turn with the causal connector *weil* followed by a subject (*die Eva*). However, instead of completing the causal clause, he inserts a couple of parenthetical remarks which express background information about the beneficiary of the request. These parenthetical remarks are independent main clauses with their finite verbs in the second position. After having provided the necessary background information, Thomas continues with his causal clause. It is in this context that the finite verb of the causal clause is positioned in the second slot. I argue that in this instance, the verb-second position functions as a cohesive device in that it aligns itself, at the syntactic level, with the preceding parenthetical remarks which also display main clause word order. Let us now examine some additional instances that exhibit the grammatical structure of the *weil*-clauses just described. Segment 5 is another example of a multi-unit account turn.

Account turn after a request receives a preferred response

(5)   Markus/Klaus (Tennisschläger)

```
39 ->  Klaus  : un   dann  kann  ich  d-dir  vielleicht  schicken  weil
                and  then  can   i    y-you  maybe       send      because
                and then i can maybe send y-you because

40 ->  Klaus  : ich hab  hier  jetzt da   ein vom ( )  der  kostet
                i   have here  now   there one from ( )  it   costs
                i   have one  here  from the     ( ) it   costs

41 ->  Klaus  : hier fast   fünfhundert mark.  .hhh
                here almost five hundred marks. .hhh
                here almost five hundred marks. .hhh
```

Similar to the previous example, the causal connector *weil* is produced and is immediately followed by a parenthetical remark. The speaker then continues his turn by uttering a causal clause (*der kostet hier fast fünfhundert mark*) which displays main clause word order. Similar to segment 1, it appears that by placing the finite verb in an early position, the speaker frames the talk-to-follow as the causal clause, thereby facilitating a cohesion between the causal connector *weil* and the following causal clause. Furthermore, by placing the finite verb of the causal *weil*-clause in the second position, the speaker allows his co-participant to project the talk-to-follow and thereby invites a possible understanding of the following talk as a causal clause. Segment 6 (from chapter 3) also illustrates a similar instance of a multi-unit account turn.

An account after a dispreferred response to a request is projectable

(6)   Markus/Nicki (Sweatshirt)

```
28    Nicki  : weil    des  was ich mir  vor drei  jahrn bei dir gekauft
               because that what i   mir  PR  ago three years at  you bought
               because the one i bought when visiting you three years

29    Nicki  : hab (.) des  is noch   einwandfrei des lieb ich auch über
               have(.) that is still  perfect     it  love i   also over
               ago (.)that is still perfect i love it over everything i

30    Nicki  : alles       nur ich mein des  is seit drei  jahren getragen und
               everything just i   mean that is for  three years  worn      and
               just mean it's been worn for three years and it's not

31    Nicki  : so   richtig äh (.) 'n dunkles blau is  des  nicht mehr oder
               so   really  uh (.) a  dark    blue is  that not   more or
               (.) really dark blue or (.) like really
```

```
32    Nicki: (.) son   richtiges jeansblau weiste   [(son)   ]
             (.) such  really    denim blue know+you [(such a)]
             uh denim blue anymore you know          [(such a)]
```

Here, the speaker initiates the account turn by the causal connector *weil*, then inserts some background information about the object which she owns and which is also similar to the one that she asked her brother to look for and to possibly purchase for her. The actual account is: *weil so richtig dunkles blau is des nicht mehr oder son richtiges jeansblau* 'because it's not like really dark blue or like really denim blue any more'. Note that the *weil*-clause displays main clause word order. As we can see, there are several clauses inserted between the causal connector *weil* and the account clause which it introduces. Again, it seems that the verb-second clause facilitates cohesion between the connector *weil*, which signals an upcoming explanation for the request, and the following causal clause which expresses the reason for the request. Furthermore, it seems that an early position of the finite verb following several clauses makes the upcoming talk more projectable to the co-participant.

However, not all accounts for request turns marked by the causal connector *weil* have a multi-unit format. Segment 2 and 4 (below) exemplify accounts for request turn formats from my corpus which display a rather simpler format, consisting of single unit verb-second *weil*-clause accounts.

(2)   Dora/Mutti (Fotos)

```
02 ->  Dora : mh °naja° äh he .hh hum. ah kannst  vielleicht der mi-na
              mh °well° uh he .hh hum. oh can+you maybe      the mi-no
              mh °well° uh he .hh hum. oh can you maybe      the mi-no

03 ->  Dora : ich schreib jetzt ihr selber    mal der Miriam mal sagen dass
              i   write   now   to her myself PT  the Miriam MP  say   that
              i'll write her myself just tell Miriam that i have

04 ->  Dora : ich fotos     hab weil    die will a      eweng was sehen.
              i   pictures have because she wants also a bit some see.
              pictures because she also wants to see some of them.
```

(4)   Dora/Carla (Schlittschuh)

```
17 -> Carla : weil   i weiss ned selbe wo    diese dinge sind
              because i know not self where these things are
              because i don't know myself where they are
```

Notice that in both examples, speakers place the finite verb in second position. Unlike the earlier examples in which there was some talk inserted between the causal connector and the causal clause, in the present example there is no background information inserted between the *weil* and the causal clause. In segment 2, the finite verb *will* 'wants', which expresses the core semantic meaning of the clause (that of a third party wanting something), is placed in the second position. In segment 4, the finite verb *weiss* 'know', which expresses the speaker's lack of knowledge where her skates might be, is placed in the second position.

The main-clause word order in *weil*-clauses in request sequences is certainly interpretable in light of Günthner's assertion that a *weil*-clause displaying main clause word order may be seen as a separate, independent clause with its own illocutionary force. The illocutionary force in this case would be providing a reason or a justification for one's dispreferred action. However, I would instead propose that this marked word order of causal *weil*-clauses in request sequences is closely related to preference organization, in that the early appearance of the finite verb carrying core semantic meaning may be interpreted as an affiliative conversational move. I propose that causal *weil*-clauses occurring in request sequences have a very specific job to do, namely providing an explanation and justification for the speaker's dispreferred action. Recall that affiliative responses such as acceptances to invitations occur early, and that disaffiliative responses to invitations, requests, or offers are delayed. Heritage (1984a) and Davidson (1984) note that disaffiliative responses have a specific design feature: they are commonly prefaced with verbal and nonverbal elements which delay the rejection component. Such a design feature permits the co-participant to forestall a rejection and possibly revise the invitation or offer (for example) to make it more acceptable to their recipient. I argue that in my corpus, these marked causal *weil*-clauses in request sequences serve to accelerate the occurrence of the finite verb which carries the key semantic meaning of an account.[8] In doing so, speakers allow their co-participant to understand the reason for their request and to possibly pursue an acceptance. In addition, the early positioning of the finite verb makes the trajectory of the account turn more projectable for the co-participant.

Overall, I noted in this section that the grammatical structure of *weil*-clauses which express an explanation for the speaker's request may display main clause word order. I demonstrated that verb-second *weil*-clauses frequently occur in multi-unit turns in which there has been some parenthetical talk inserted between the causal connector *weil* and its clause. I argued that in such multi-unit account turns, placing the verb in the second position in *weil*-clauses may serve as a resource for projecting the developing course of the unfolding account turn-shape, thereby facilitating the recipient's understanding of the account turn and where it is going. In addition, I showed instances of single-unit causal *weil*-clauses in request sequences which display main clause word order. I argued that by positioning the verb in the second position, speakers accelerate the occurrence of the core semantic expression which may facilitate understanding of the account. This particular design of account for request appears to be "other-attentive" (Heritage 1988: 137): finite verb's placement in second position in the causal *weil*-clauses and its two interactional jobs, namely the facilitation of the co-participant's understanding of a multi-unit account turn and the early production of the item which carries the core meaning of an account for the co-participant, may be understood as strategies which address the co-participant's face as early as possible. It seems that this design for accounts is best interpreted as an affiliative strategy which supports social solidarity.

Accounts for requests may also be introduced by the coordinating conjunction of *denn* 'because'. The following section provides a description of such instances.

4.5. Accounts for request turns marked by the coordinating conjunction "denn" 'because'

The majority of accounts in request sequences in the corpus are introduced by the causal connector *weil*. It was previously illustrated that all *weil*-clauses in the data share a common grammatical structure, i.e., they all display main clause word order (finite verb in second position) – a feature which is specific to spoken discourse. The causal connector *weil*, however, is not the only lexeme in German which marks causal relationships between clauses. The coordinating conjunction *denn* 'because' also links clauses causally (Duden 1998; Eisenberg 1986). Unlike *weil*, the formal word order for *denn*-clauses is main clause word order. Another distinction between *weil* und *denn* is that *denn* is positionally restricted, in that it can only refer to a preceding statement (Engel 1991). In other words, a *denn*-clause cannot be pre-positioned; this is a feature which was also suggested for verb-second *weil*-clauses.[9] Studies on the usage of *weil* and *denn* in everyday conversation note that these two conjunctions are not interchangeable in German. In general, linguists propose that Germans tend to use *weil* more often in spoken language, and *denn* in written or formal language, to mark a causal relationship between clauses (Günthner 1993, 1996; Pasch 1997; Schlobinski 1992; Uhmann 1996). These researchers further suggest that the lexeme *denn* is being replaced by the causal connector *weil* in the spoken language.[10] As a matter of fact, Günthner (1993, 1996) suggests that in all her examples of *weil*-clauses which perform accounts for speech acts, the causal connector *weil* can be substituted by *denn* without semantically changing the causal clause.

Out of 30 instances of requests sequences in my corpus, speakers used the coordinating conjunction *denn* to mark the account for their requests only twice. Segment 6 illustrates one of the instances. This data fragment is taken from a telephone conversation between two friends: Markus, a German student in an exchange program in the United States; and his friend, Peter, a dentist in Germany. Since this request sequence is rather extensive, only turns that are relevant to the phenomenon under discussion have been provided. The exchanges marked by arrows involve a kind of giving an account for a request (lines 33, 35, 37–39, 41). This is the context in which the pre-request, request and the account for request occur: Prior to the beginning of the data segment, the two speakers discuss Peter's wedding in the summer to which Markus is invited. The conversation continues with Markus informing his friend that he will be able to go to the wedding since it is going to be during the time he will be in Germany.

(6)   Markus/Peter (Zahn)

```
01      Markus : =ja ganz     genau und mir fehlen zwei zähne und deswegen
                 =yes totally exact and i   miss    two  teeth and therefore
                 =yea exactly and i'm missing two teeth and therefore

02      Markus : will ich auch zu dir kommen hehehe=
                 want i    also to you come    hehehe=
                 i also want to come and see you hehehe=

03      Peter  : =ach ja  wie  wollen wir das  jetzt machen?
                 =oh  yes how  want   we  that now   do?
                 =oh yea how do we want to do that?

04      Markus : du  ich hab  ähm hinten in   ähm in ähm (.).hh der letzte
                 you i   have uhm back   in   uhm in uhm (.).hh the last
                 you i   have uhm in the back uhm in uhm (.)    the last

05      Markus : der letzte zahn  im im unterkiefer im ( ) und da     hab  ich
                 the last    tooth in in lower jaw   in ( ) and there have i
                 the last tooth in in the lower jaw in ( ) and there i

06      Markus : ähm (.) jetzt (.) n loch drin     im ….
                 uhm (.) now   (.) a hole in the in …
                 have uhm (.) a hole in the in…

                    .

                    .

                    .


20               (0.8)

21      Markus : hab ich was  bekommen?
                 have i   what received?
                 have i received what?

22      Peter  : root canal filling?

23               (.)
```

```
24    Markus : ne: das   hab  ich noch nicht bekommen. .hhh aber was  ich
               no: that  have i   yet  not   received. .hhh but  what i
               no: i haven't had a root canal filling yet. .hhh but what

25    Markus : nu:r  ähm wenn du   wenn du  zeit hast.=ja?
               o:nly uhm  if  you if   you  time have.=yea?
               i o:nly uhm if you if you have time.=yea?

26    Peter  : [ja
               [yes
               [yea
               [
27    Markus:  [also wenn du  natürlich da   .hhh b-beschäftigt zu
               [but  if   you naturally there .hhh b-busy       too
               [but of course if you're .hhh too b-busy

28    Markus : beschäftigt bist und dann ä:h .hhh m-m-muss's nicht sein
               busy        are  and then u:h .hhh m-m-must   not   be
               and then u:h .hhh it d-d-does not have to be

29    Markus : aber (.) das   dann  du   könntst vielleicht mal gucken und
               but  (.) that  then  you  could   maybe      MP  look   and
               but  (.) that  then  you  could   maybe take a  look at it

30    Markus : mir nur   sagen was  was  vielleicht (.)ä:h gemacht werden
               me  only  say   what what maybe     (.) u:h done    will
               and only tell me what what maybe (.) u:h has to be

31 -> Markus : müsste   ba [ld .hhh [denn   ähm denn  `n zahnarzt ich-k (.)
               mustSUB  so [on .hhh [because uhm because a dentist  i-k  (.)
               done     so [on .hhh [because uhm because a dentist i-k (.)
                            [           [
32 -> Peter  :              [mh,     [mh,
                            [mh,     [mh,
                            [mh,     [mh,

33 -> Markus : der damals als ich bei mei-bei dem  bei unserm zahnarzt
               who then   as  i   at  my-at   whom at  our    dentist
               who then as i went to my-to whom saw our dentist,

34 -> Markus : war,[.hhh zu dem   meine ganze familie immer  hingegangen
               was,[.hhh to whom  my    whole family always PRX+went
                   [.hhh to whom my whole family always
                   [
35    Peter  :      [mh,
                    [mh,
                    [mh,

36 -> Markus : ist und auch der kieferorthopäde die  ham mir da    ja im
               AUX and also the orthodontist    they AUX me  there MP in
               went and also the orthodontist they pocked

37 -> Markus : mund rumgedoktort? :  .h[hh und ähm ham  sachen
               mouth arounddoctored? .h[hh and uhm have stuff
```

```
                       around in my mouth?    .h[hh and uhm did
                                               [
39       Peter    :                           [mh,
                                               [mh,
                                               [mh,


38 -> Markus    gemacht die ich gar  nicht gebraucht hab. .hhh
                done which I at all   not needed have. .hhh
                some stuff that i didn't need at all. .hhh


39       Peter   : ach so,?
                   oh  really,?
                   oh  really ?


40       Markus  : ich hab ähm=
                   i have uhm=
                   i have uhm=


41       Peter   : =hat  sich das  nacher rausgeste [llt?
                   =have RXP  that later    PRX+     [found?
                   =did that turned out to be the case [later?
                                                       [
42       Markus:                                     [ja ja
                                                     [yes yes
                                                     [yea yea


43              (.)


44       Markus  : .hhh der zahnarzt hat mich zum kieferorthopäden
                   .hhh the dentist AUX  RXP to   orthodontist
                   .hhh the dentist sent me to see an orthodontist
                   .
                   .
                   .
                   .


97       Markus  : [.hhh und ähm und und hab dann mal gesehen was   der ähm
                   [.hhh and uhm and and AUX then MP   seen     what the uhm
                   [.hhh and uhm and and saw  it once what the uhm


98       Markus  : (0.2) also die unterschiede un  konnte   mal vergleichen
                   (0.2) so   the differences and could     MP  compare
                   (0.2) so   the differences and was able to  compare


99       Markus  : und was der andere zahnarzt da     noch  gemeint hat und .hhh
                   and what the other dentist   there still meant   AUX and .hhh
                   and what the other dentist   thought and .hhh


100      Markus  : und ähm deswegen (.) das kann ich das kann ich selbst
                   and uhm therefore (.) that can i that can i self
                   and uhm therefore (.) i can i cannot judge it


101      Markus  : nicht beurteilen, [.hh und dann ähm (0.2) ist das  ganz
                   not judge,        [.hh and then uhm (0.2) is  that quite
```

```
            all by myself,   [.hh and then uhm (0.2) it's quite
                             [
102   Peter  :               [mh,
                             [mh,
                             [mh,

103   Markus : gut  dass du   zahnarzt bist gell?  he:: hehe [.hhh
               good that you  dentist  are  right? he:: hehe [.hhh
               good that you're a dentist  right? he::hehe [.hhh
                                                           [
104   Peter  :                                             [ja, ist kein
                                                           [yes, is no
                                                           [yes, no

105   Peter  : problem du kannst ähm (0.2) wir können ja irgendiwe
               problem you can   uhm (0.2) we could  MP somehow
               problem you can uhm (0.2) we could somehow make

106   Peter  : schon  mal `n termin       ausmachen…
               already MP  an appointment arrange…
               an appointment already…
```

Shortly before this segment the co-participants started to talk about Markus' recent motorcycle accident, and make jokes about Markus' looks on a motorcycle: on a Harley Davidson wearing a leather pants and supposedly with missing teeth. Following this telling, Markus makes a pre-request (lines 1–2) which takes the form of mentioning missing teeth (jokingly). It should be mentioned that during an earlier telephone conversation, Markus and Peter had talked about the possibility of Peter examining Markus' teeth during Markus' visit in Germany. Peter in turn responds first with *ach ja* 'oh yea' thus displaying his recognition of the topic from their earlier conversation, and moves into making arrangements by uttering *wie wollen wir das jetzt mach?* 'how do we want to do that?' (line 3). Instead of responding to Peter's inquiry, Markus in turn explains some of the problems he has been having with the fillings in his teeth (only lines 4–6 included in the transcript). Markus' description of his dental problems seems to be doing some remedial work for his pre-request or previous request during what is surely a busy time for Peter (it is shortly before his wedding). At one point in Markus' description of his dental problem, Peter asks whether he has received a particular treatment (line 24). Peter's question almost sounds like an examination over the phone. This is followed by a repair sequence, at which time Markus performs a request (lines 25, 27–31). Note that Markus' request turn is full of disfluencies, suggesting that he views his request request as problematic. Also, he begins his request utterance with a conditional *wenn*-clause expressing the condition according to which he wishes his request to be complied with (line 24). Recall that Peter is getting married during Markus' visit in Germany; Markus makes his request even though it might be a busy time for his friend. Thus, Markus' request turn design seems to display orientation to the possible problem with compliance of his request. Following his request, Markus continues his turn with an account for his request (lines 31, 33, 34, 36–37). Note that immediately following his request and after an inbreath, Markus produces the conjunction *denn*. In doing so, he signals that the upcoming talk will be some sort of an explanation. He continues his turn with an explanation that the dental treatments that he actually received from their family dentist and the orthodontist were not necessary. When comparing this instance of an account for a request marked by *denn* with the previous examples of account for requests, we can note some features that both types of account design share. For example, similar to the account turns which were marked by the causal connector *weil*, the request and account turn in this example is a multi-unit. The speaker in this data segment also inserts parenthetical information (the dentist to whom the whole family goes) between the causal connector *denn* and the clause which expresses the account. The composition of the account in this example also displays some "no fault" quality in that it refers to the maltreatment of the speaker by other dentists. In sum, this example of an account for request shares many features with the examples of *weil*-clauses as accounts for requests discussed previously. In this example, it even appears that we could replace *denn* with *weil* without changing the meaning of the account utterance. This example corresponds with Günthner's suggestion that the connector *denn* is being replaced by the causal connector *weil* in spoken German. However, as I noted earlier there are only two instances of *denn*-clauses in my collection of request sequences. Additionally, the rare occurrence of the conjunction *denn* in spoken discourse means that they do not lend themselves to close study. In the next section, I discuss instances in which speakers provide an account for their request without explicitly marking it.

4.6. Accounts provided for requests without being prefaced by a conjunction

So far, I have examined cases in which speakers offer an explanation for their request and in which they explicitly mark their explanation by the causal connector *weil*. I have also discussed the one of the two instances of an account for a request turn in my corpus which is marked by the connector *denn*. In this section, I discuss instances in which speakers produce an account for their request without explicitly marking it by a causal connector. The next data segment (7) illustrates such an instance. This is a conversation between Karin, a German speaker who at the time was a student at an American university, and her sister-in-law in Germany, who is planning to come and visit her in the United States.

(7)   Karin/Rita (Pflaumenmuss)

```
01    Karin  : .hhh oka:y,
               .hhh oka:y,
               .hhh oka:y,


02    Rita   : >okay< kar[in
               >okay< kar[in
               >okay< kar[in
                          [
03    Karin  : [du übrigens  weisst    du  was  wenn ihr
               [you by the way know+you you what when you
               [by  the way you know what when you


04    Karin  : ähm m   winter kommt, (0.7) .hh da bringt mir
               uhm in winter come,  (0.7) .hh MP bring   me
               uhm come to visit in winter, (0.7).hh MP bring


05    Karin  : pflaumenmus pflaumemus mit
               plum jam    plum jam  with
               me plum jam plum jam


06               (0.5)


07    Rita   : [hä:,?
               [hu:,?
               [hu:,?
               [
08    Karin  : [e:h he he he he .HHH ich ha(h)b  heute morgen den
               [u:h he he he he .HHH i   ha(h)ve today morning the
               [u:h he he he he .HHH this morning i finished the


09    Karin  : letzten pflaumenmus verspeist. ist    schon   ganz
               last    plum jam    ate.       it is already completely
               last    plum jam. it's quite


10    Karin  : traurig he he [he he he
               sad he he     [he he he
               sad he he     [he he he


11    Rita   : [kann man den kann man den auch
               [can one it  can one it   also
               [can you can you also


12    Rita   : schicken,? [(    )
               send,?     [(    )
               mail it,?  [
```

In lines 3–5, Karin asks her sister-in-law to bring her more plum jam from Germany (a kind of jam that is not available in the United States) when she visits her in winter. After a pause (line 6), Karin provides her recipient with some explanation for her request, i.e., the fact that she had finished the last of her plum jam that morning. Note that the pause after Karin's request may have been understood by her as indication of some possible dispreferred response. Therefore, Karin's account can be interpreted as making her request more acceptable. Note also that Rita's non-specified repair, which is in overlap with the beginning of Karin's account turn, may be interpreted as addressing aspects of the sequential connection rather than the request turn itself. In other words, Karin's request does not seem to be topically linked to the prior turn and therefore it might seem unexpected and unconnected to Rita. Note that unlike the previous examples of account for request, the account in this request sequence is not marked by a causal connector *weil*. Gohl (2000) notes that in her corpus, speakers frequently link their accounts for actions asyndetically, i.e., through producing an account without explicitly linking it to the utterance that it is providing the account for (p. 83). She suggests that a first indication of the connectivity of asyndetically-linked utterances is their sequential proximity (Gohl 2000: 84). She further notes, however, that not only the sequential proximity, but also the meaning and contextual aspects of utterances contribute to any implicit connection between them (p. 87). Looking at the above data segment, the content and placement of Karin's turn (lines 8 and 9) suggest that it is to be understood as an account. By providing some explanation for her request, which has received some hesitant responses, the speaker pursues an acceptance from her recipient. Note also that this turn is in the sequential proximity of a request. Some design features that this account turn shares with the other discussed examples are: (a) similar to all the previous examples of accounts for requests, the account in this example refers to the lack of access to the requested object. The speaker in this data segment has just finished the last jar of plum jam, a German food item not available in the United States. Thus it appears that this account, similar to the other ones discussed in this chapter, carries a "no fault" quality; (b) compared to some of the previous examples of accounts for requests which were marked by the causal connector *weil,* this example of an account turn type is a single unit turn, which makes the turn rather short. In other words, the speaker does not insert additional background information into the account turn. Gohl (2000) notes that most of the instances of accounts for requests in her corpus are not typically marked by causal connectors such as *weil*.[11] The majority of accounts for request instances in my corpus, however, suggest a tendency for account utterances to be explicitly marked by the causal connector *weil.* Additionally, the majority of these cases consist of multiple units.

4.7. Discussion

The investigation of the organization of accounts for requests has demonstrated that their sequential placement, content and grammatical structure are tightly connected to preference organization and maintenance of social solidarity. The following is a summary and discussion of the salient interactional functions performed by these specific features of accounts for requests and which were explicated in this chapter.

Heritage (1984a, 1988) noted that accounts are socially institutionalized features and are normatively given or demanded in contexts in which the projected or next relevant action does not occur, and that their design and placement are strongly connected to the management of self-other relationships. This chapter showed that accounts are usually given in request sequences. Requests are face-threatening activities because they put some obligation on the recipient (Brown and Levinson 1979; Goffman 1955; Lerner 1996a); thus, when making a request, speakers frequently give an account for their face-threatening act. In this chapter, I showed that accounts for requests are not only given in a context in which the projected preferred action does not occur, but that they are also produced in a context in which the preferred action has already occurred. I argued that while accounts for requests serve to maintain social relationships and social solidarity, their different sequential placements within the request sequence appear to perform different interactional functions. The chapter explicated that accounts which were placed in a context where a dispreferred response was projectable were used to pursue an acceptance as a preferred next action from their recipients. On the other hand, accounts which were produced after the recipient had already accepted to comply with the request functioned more as remedial work. Put differently, such accounts were used in order to repair the damage that the face-threatening act of request may have caused to the recipient's face.

Sequential placements of accounts were not the only features found to be connected to issues of face. The analysis of the content of accounts for requests in the German corpus suggested that accounts which German speakers provided for their dispreferred action of requests frequently referred to some "uncontrollable" issue and/or "lack of access" to the requested object. In other words, speakers designed their accounts for requests in such a way as to address "no fault" (Heritage 1984a) issues, implicating a circumstance which was out of the speaker's control or implying that the speaker could not perform the requested service themselves. I argued that similar to accounts in dispreferred responses, the "no fault" quality of accounts for requests serves to avoid threatening the co-participant's face and the co-participant's relationship, thus maintaining social solidarity. I also argued that speakers frequently provided background information in their account turns in order to make their request not only more understandable, but also more accept-able, thereby avoiding any threat to the social relationship between themselves and their co-participants.

The chapter also provided a discussion of the grammatical structure of accounts for requests in German conversation and illustrated how specific syntactical struc-tures of account utterances function as affiliative moves. While analyzing accounts for requests with respect to their grammatical structure, it became apparent that they are frequently introduced by the causal connector *weil* and that they display main-clause word order. As such, the word order of these *weil*-clauses is marked; they may therefore be interpretable as separate independent clauses with their own illocutionary force and which mitigate the face threatening act of request. In addition, I argued that the earlier placement of the finite verb in accounts for request utterances may be understood as an affiliative move in two ways. It was demonstrated that the early placement of the finite verb has to do with account turn cohesion: by placing the verb in the second position, speakers may make a rather elaborative account turn more cohesive for their co-participants. Addition-ally, I argued that an early placement of the finite verb in an account utterance marked by the causal connector *weil* can accelerate the occurrence of the finite verb which carries the core semantic meaning of the account utterance. Further-more, I argued that the causal connector *weil* and the second-position of the finite verb provide co-participants with resources for anticipating both what kind of action is under construction, and what it will take to be completed.

In the last part of the chapter, I showed that accounts for requests may also be marked by the causal connector *denn*; however, in my corpus *denn* was used as a causal connector less frequently than *weil*. This is in accordance with the findings of researchers who have looked at the occurrences of *denn* as a causal connector in spoken language. Furthermore, I discussed accounts for requests which speakers may produce without explicitly marking them by a causal connector. In such instances, it seems that not only the sequential proximity but also the contextual (including semantic) aspects of utterances contribute to the understanding of a turn and an account for a request.

In this chapter, we saw how the sequential placement, content and gram-matical structures of one specific action, viz. giving an account for a request, seem to be influenced by the underlying structure of social interaction, i.e., the manage-ment of self-and other relationships and the maintenance of social solidarity. The next chapter deals with how speakers provide their co-participants with resources for projecting an upcoming request sequence.

Notes

1. I use the term "causal connector" which has been used by Ford and Mori (1994) to refer to the lexical item "weil", since the term "causal connector" seems to refer to the action such conjunctions perform rather than its prescribed grammatical function.

2. Antaki (1994) provides one example of an instance in which an account is provided following a pre-request. In the example, Antaki notes that the speaker's pre-request signals that what comes next might be hearable as an imposition, and that therefore the speaker provides an account before actually making the request (p. 87). Antaki does not mention, however, whether this particular placement of account delays the production of the projected request.

3. In her comprehensive study of adverbial clauses in American English conversations, Ford (1993) found that in every case, the causal clauses in her corpus (including *because*-clauses) appeared only after the material they modified (p. 64).

4. Ford and Thompson (1996) suggest in their discussion of interactional units in conversation the notion of "pragmatic completion" which refers to "utterances that may be interpreted as a complete conversational action within its specific sequential context" (p. 150).

5. However, in his analysis of the usage of German *weil* in the spoken language, Scheutz demonstrates that there are discrepancies with this hypothesis that verb-second *weil*-clauses are limited to epistemic causality while verb-final *weil*-clauses are used for expressing propositional causal relationships.

6. Günthner (1996) is the only researcher that I am aware of who discusses sequential placements in which *weil*-clauses with marked word order occur.

7. The effect of this syntactic structure upon the projectability of structures and the placement of possible completions in German is briefly addressed by Ochs et al. (1996). This phenomenon needs further research.

8. Of course, this is an argument for *weil*-clauses with marked word order in request sequences. We also need to examine *weil*-clauses in other dispreferred actions to see whether we can observe a similar marked word order.

9. Note that verb-final *weil*-clauses may be placed in either pre- or post-position, i.e. before or after the main clause.

10. Many studies have suggested a regional difference in the usage of *denn* and *weil*. However, the more recent studies have shown that the disappearance of *denn* in spoken German is related not to regional dialects, but rather to the context of spoken discourse. For detailed discussion of the usage of *denn* and *weil* in the

German language see Schlobinski 1992; Scheutz 1998; Küper 1984; Pasch 1997; Uhmann 1996, 1998; Wegener 1993.

11. Gohl (2000) proposes that asyndetic linkage seems to occur in particular environments. For example, it seems that they are preferred to conjunctional linkage in cases of interactively produced constructions. Another preferred circumstance is when an account refers to a non-verbal action: in such cases, there is no previous utterance or implication to which a conjunctional clause could be linked. Overall, it seems that more studies are needed to examine the causal relationship between utterances and the circumstances in which they tend to be produced.

CHAPTER 5

Initiating request sequences: The design of request sequence turn beginnings

5.1. Introduction

In the previous two chapters, I focused on the linguistic design of pre-request and request utterances. In chapter 3 I offered a description of how turns at talk are understood by their recipient as pre-requests by virtue of their design and placement and how, together with their subsequent talk, they occasion the activity of requests. In chapter 4 I provided a description of the design and sequential placement of accounts in request sequences with a focus on the interactional function they serve in request sequences. The present chapter is concerned with the talk that occurs prefatory to pre-request or request utterances. Specifically, this chapter provides a description of how speakers construct their next turn as introducing a new sequence of requesting. Moreover, the chapter demonstrates that speakers employ various linguistic units as special interactional devices to mark their request sequence as a new activity, thereby allowing their co-participant to not only project what action is being performed at the moment, but also the type of action(s) which is supposed to follow.

In the next section, I first provide a discussion of topical organization and projectability of actions, two conversation analytical notions that play an important role in analyzing prefatory components to pre-request and request turns presented in this chapter. I will then continue with a discussion of the linguistic construction of utterances prefatory to pre-request and request turns which mark the beginning of the new activity of requesting in the ongoing talk in German conversation.

5.2. On the sequential organization of topical talk

It has been noted that when speakers enter a conversation, they regularly have a specific item or topic that they want to tell their co-participant. However, speakers usually don't begin the conversation with that specific item; instead, they allow the "mentionable" item to be something that comes up "naturally" in the course of the ongoing conversation (Schegloff and Sacks 1973; Sacks 1996). In their discussion of topic organization, Schegloff and Sacks suggest "fitting" as a preferred procedure:

> ...That is, it appears that a preferred way of getting mentionables mentioned is to employ the resources of the local organization of utterances in the course of the conversation. That involves holding off the mention of a mentionable until it can occur "naturally", that is, until it can be fitted to another conversationalist's prior utterance, allowing his utterance to serve as a sufficient source for the mentioning of the mentionable...   (Schegloff and Sacks 1973: 301)

While speakers may begin a conversation with a specific mentionable in mind and refrain from mentioning it until the appropriate moment, Jefferson's (1984b) study on topic transition shows that new topics may also be occasioned by some item that was mentioned in the previous talk. In general, research on the sequential organization of topical talk has shown that speakers have resources available which allow them to close a topical item and introduce a new one (Button 1990; Button and Casey 1984; Drew and Holt 1998; Goodwin and Goodwin 1992; Jefferson 1984b; Maynard 1980; Schegloff 1996; Schegloff and Sacks 1973). Overall, two common practices for moving from one topic to another have been proposed (Sacks 1996, Jefferson 1984b). One involves a gradual disengagement from the old topic to the new one. Sacks (1996) refers to this type of topic transition as a "stepwise" move during which speakers gradually link up the new topic with the preceding one (566). Speakers may also move from talking about one topic to another in a rather abrupt and disjunctive way. In this process, speakers close one topic and begin a new topic without linking up the new topic to the previous one (Jefferson 1984b: 198). The above mentioned studies on talk-in-interaction focusing on topic organization have revealed that speakers perform these transitions (i.e., the stepwise or abrupt shifts from one topic to another) in a rather organized and coordinated manner. For example, the findings of these studies demonstrate that speakers employ various linguistic expressions as an interactional strategy to close a topic and move to some other activity. Drew and Holt's (1998) study on the sequential distribution of "figurative expressions" in conversation illustrates that such expressions occur frequently in topic transition sequences, thereby initiating the closing of a topic.[1] Speakers may also utilize specific linguistic expressions in order to bring up items which may be sequentially out of place. These may be topical items which were just brought to the speaker's mind. In such instances, by using a "misplacement marker" (Schegloff and Sacks 1973: 319) such as "by the way", speakers display to their co-participants their understanding of what they are doing, i.e., introducing a new topic which does not naturally fit with the previous utterance. Naturally, central to the management of moving from the activity of topical talk to another activity is the notion of projectability. The following section provides a description of this concept.

5.3. Projectability of actions

Schegloff (1988) notes that "parties to real conversations are always talking in some sequential context" (61). The term "sequential context" refers to the inter-actional environment in which the current speaker's unfolding turn is placed. Because of this interactional environment, the speaker's unfolding turn may be projectable by the preceding talk and at the same time, the speaker's unfolding turn may be projecting further talk and action. Considering this particular feature of an unfolding turn, it seems that the grammatical structure of that turn becomes one fundamental resource for speakers which allows them to inspect their co-participant's unfolding turn design and to "foreshadow" (Sacks et al. 1974) the trajectory of the ongoing action before it has been fully performed. This is not limited to projecting the ongoing action, but also encompasses foreshadowing the kind of subsequent action to expect. Simply said, the grammatical structure of utterances in a turn provides information about the unfolding turn and the subse-quent talk/action which may be developed. In recent years, a number of studies have focused on the relationship between grammar and projection by exploring various aspects of talk-in-interaction in English and other languages (Auer 2005; Ford, Fox and Thompson 2002; Goodwin 1980, 1981; Hayashi 2003; Lerner 1991, 1996a, 1996b, 2002; Sacks et al. 1974; Streeck 1995). In general, these studies have demonstrated that projectability is one of the fundamental resources that facilitate close coordination and collaboration between speakers in interaction.

One feature in talk-in-interaction that is central to the notion of project-ability is the *preface*. Prefaces are components or types of talk that are produced "prefatory" or "preliminary" to other talk that might follow and are treated by the recipient as prefaces or as talk that "leads up" to the projected action (Schegloff and Sacks 1973; Schegloff 1980). Prefaces may range from rather minimal components such as *well*, or lexical items such as *listen*, to complete utterances such as *can I ask you a favor*? (Schegloff 1980). Prefatory utterances such as *I wanna tell you something* or *can I ask you a favor*? have specific interactional features in that they project some specific type of action which is usually mentioned in the utterance. Furthermore, the projected action does not occur in the utterance, but is instead mentioned by the name of the action or by a pronoun in the utterance. Schegloff (1980: 110) refers to this type of utterance as an "action projection". However, as Schegloff demonstrates in his paper "preliminaries to preliminaries" (1980), action projection utterances are not always followed by the projected action: there may be some other talk between the action projection and the action that can be understood as talk prefaced to the projected action, which may serve as a kind of preparatory work for the action. In such a case, the talk between the action projection and the action can serve as prefatory or "preliminary" to the action, and thus the action projection may be understood as preliminaries to preliminaries or "pre-pre's" (Schegloff 1980: 116). In sum, then, what is followed by the pre-pre's is preliminary to the action that they project.

In the above sections, I discussed the notions of topical talk and project-ability of turns and actions. These are two aspects of talk-in-interaction which are central to the investigation of the sequential context in which request sequences are produced, in particular, the way in which they are occasioned and initiated in the course of the ongoing conversation. In the following section, I will demonstrate that requests may be occasioned by some matters which were mentioned in previous talk. They may also be items which were held off until the speaker found the right moment in the conversation to perform his/her request. While discussing the interactional environment in which speakers perform a request, I will focus on the steps speakers take in order to initiate their new request sequence. I will do this through exploring the construction of speakers' pre-request and/or request turn beginnings.

5.4. The sequential context in which requests occur: Steps speakers take to initiate their new activity of requesting

The present section provides a description of the sequential context in which speakers may perform their request. In particular, the analysis will focus on instances of requests which were brought to the speaker's mind by items in the previous talk. Furthermore, this section will offer a description of the linguistic resources speakers utilize to perform their request in relation to the sequential context.

Similar to any other types of talk, request sequences may be occasioned by an utterance that was produced earlier in the talk. For example, a request may be a part of an answer to a question:

(1)   (Doppelkopf, 0:07:40:00)[2]

```
1     A   : soll    sie das   hier  draußn  trinkn  könn?  [oder solls-
              should  she that  here  outside drink   can?   [or should s-
              should he be able to drink this here outside [or should
                                                           [
2     S   :                                                [NEne↑
                                                           [Nono↑
                                                           [Nono↑
```

```
3 ->   S    : stells    ihr  drinne hin  °wo's     stand°.
             Put+it  for  her  inside down °where+it stood°.
             put it down for her inside °where it was°.
```

In response to A's question (line 1), S responds negatively first, then asks A to put the water bowl for the dog inside. Here, the request is occasioned by the question in the preceding turn. This is the sequential context in which this request is produced. The activity of requesting may also be occasioned by some topical talk in prior turns. Similar to any mentionable items, speakers may enter a conversation with a particular request in mind and hold off performing it until they reach the naturally fitted place in the course of the conversation. The next data fragment exemplifies such an instance. Recall that this is a conversation between two friends: Markus, a German student in an exchange program in the United States; and his friend, Peter, a dentist in Germany. This request sequence involves Markus asking his dentist friend to examine his teeth during his visit to Germany (see analysis for data fragment 6 in chapter 4). Note that during an earlier telephone conversation, the two friends had talked about the possibility of Peter examining his friend's teeth.

(2) Markus/Peter (Zahn)

```
01     Markus  :      [ne: hehehe naja ich hab  die harley und dann
                      [no: hehehe well i   have the harley and then
                      [no: hehehe well i have the harley and then

02     Markus  : die lederhosen    und dann die äh skull cap und äh hehehe=
                  the leather+pants and then the uh skull cap and uh hehehe=
                  leather pants and then the uh skull cap and uh hehehe=

03     Peter   : =mittlerweile    lange haare und so
                  =in the meanwhile long  hair  and so
                  =in the meantime long hair and so on

04 ->  Markus  : =ja  ganz    genau und mir fehlen zwei zähne und deswegen
                  =yes totally exact and i   miss   two  teeth and therefore
                  =yeah exactly and i'm missing two teeth and therefore

05 ->  Markus  : will ich auch zu dir kommen hehehe=
                  want i    also to you come   hehehe=
                  i also want to come and see you hehehe=

06 ->  Peter   : =ach ja  wie wollen wir das  jetzt machen?
                  =oh  yes how want   we  that now   do?
                  =oh yeah how do we want to do that?
```

The context in which Markus performs his pre-request is that of topical talk about Markus' recent motorcycle accident, which is then developed into a joke about him on a Harley Davidson wearing leather pants and a skull cap, and having long hair. It is in this context that Markus mentions another feature, namely missing teeth (jokingly). This telling by Markus is understood by his co-participant as a pre-request (see his response in line 6). Note that Markus' pre-request is produced in an environment in which the previous talk involved describing Markus' looks as a would-be Harley Davidson rider. It is in this sequential context that Markus utters the pre-request. It appears that this is the place with the most natural fit for Markus' request sequence initiation.

While examining the instances of request sequences in my corpus, it became clear that about half of the requests were introduced into the conversation as items which had just been brought to the speaker's mind (i.e., the requester). As such, their turn beginnings exhibit a particular grammatical construction which marks the introduction of a new activity. Interactionally speaking, the prefatory components which occupy the pre-request and/or request turn beginnings can generally mark the turn as the beginning of a new activity without revealing any specifics about the type of action the unfolding turn will perform. Utterances prefatory to pre-request and/or requests may also be designed in such a way that they not only mark the turn as the beginning of a new sequence, but also provide some specific information about the type of activity that will be performed either at the end of the turn or in the subsequent talk. In the following subsections I provide examples of such instances of request sequence prefatory talk. The discussion begins with examples of rather generally marking a new activity, and moves to examples which illustrate how a speaker's choice of linguistic expressions may provide specific information about the type of activity that will follow.

5.4.1   "Non-specific" prefatory components to request utterances

In this subsection, I describe instances of request sequences which have been introduced by the speaker, i.e., the requester, as an item that has just been brought to their mind. In such an instance, speakers use interactional devices to abruptly shift the talk to perform the request that they just remembered. Furthermore, the turn which contains the request utterance may be designed to mark the introduction of a new activity without giving any specific information to the co-participant about the type of activity that will follow. The next data fragment exemplifies an instance of a request sequence which is introduced as a new topic/sequence. Note that the request turn in this data segment has already been discussed in chapter 4. Here, I examine the linguistic components placed in the initial position of a turn which begins a new sequence of requesting. Recall that this is a phone conversation between Tina and her mother and that some point in the course of their conversation, Tina asks her mother to look for a document on their computer at home. Prior to the beginning of the request sequence, Tina's mother told her that her father would be participating in a city hiking event. In response, Tina says *klingt gut* 'sounds good' and after a micro pause, begins a new turn which is the beginning of a new sequence of requesting (line 3).

    (3)   Tina/Mutti (Dokument)

```
01      Tina    : kling gut.
                  sounds good.
                  sounds good.

02              (.)

03 ->   Tina    : .hhh a:h ah mensch pass   mal auf wenn's    mal
                  .hhh o:h oh man       watch MP   SUF when you MP
                  .hhh o:h oh man listen the next time you get

04      Tina    : wieder anen    computer gehst. [mh?
                  again   to the computer  go.   [mh?
                  to the computer.              [mh?
                                                [
05      Mutti   :                              [mhm,
                                              ⌐ [mhm,
                                                [mhm,

06      Tina    : suchauftrag.
                  searching task.
                  searching task.

07              (0.5)

08      Mutti   : mh,
                  mh,
                  mh,
```

In line 3, Tina begins a new turn with an audible inbreath and a series of *ahs* 'oh'. She then continues, uttering the lexical item *mensch* 'man' and the linguistic expression *pass mal auf* 'listen'. It seems that these elements occupying the initial position of Tina's request turn serve a particular interactional function. Schegloff (1984: 38) notes that speakers may begin an utterance with an "oh" when the utterance is not topically linked to the talk before and thereby mark the utterance that follows as "unplanned" or disjunctive. It appears that the *a:h* in Tina's turn can be interpreted as such a disjunction marker.[3] In Tina's turn the speech token *a:h* is followed by *mensch* 'man', a summons and the phrase *pass mal auf* 'listen' which literally means pay attention. Similar to English "hey" and "listen" when they occur as markers in new topic turn initial position (Schegloff 1980: 140), in Tina's turn *mensch* and *pass mal auf* appear to be signaling a new topic, in this case, a new sequence to come. And as we can see, Tina continues her turn with her request. In sum, elements such as *ah, mensch,* and *pass mal auf* may be placed in the initial position of the new request initiation turn which: (a) mark the beginning of a new activity; (b) mark that what the speaker is about to perform is not related to prior talk, and (c) project more talk to come. However, these markers do *not* indicate *which* type of action is about to be performed.

The next data fragment exemplifies another instance of an abrupt move to the new activity of request. As we can note, here the request turn is initiated with a series of prefatory components which project an immediate and abrupt topic shift. Similar to the previous data segment, the prefatory units in this instance of request utterance do not provide the recipient with any information regarding the type of the projected activity. The data fragment is taken from a conversation between a German student, Karin, who is on an exchange program in the United States and her sister-in-law, Rita, in Germany. Karin asks her sister-in-law to bring her plum jam from Germany when she visits her in the United States (lines 3–4). Note that her request is sequentially out of place in that it is uttered in an environment in which speakers have just performed a set of pre-closing units (Schegloff and Sacks 1973).

(4)   Karin/Rita (Pflaumenmus)

```
01      Karin   :   .hhh oka:y,
                    .hhh oka:y,
                    .hhh oka:y,

02      Rita    :   >okay< kar[in
                    >okay< kar[in
                    >okay< kar[in
                              [
03 ->   Karin   :         [du übrigens   weisst   du   was   wenn   ihr
                          [you by the way know+you you  what  when  you
                          [by the way you know what when you

04 ->   Karin   :   ähm `m winter kommt, (0.7) .hh da bringt mir
                    uhm in winter come,  (0.7) .hh MP bring me
                    uhm come to visit in winter, (0.7).hh MP bring

05 ->   Karin   :   pflaumenmus pflaumemus mit
                    plum jam    plum jam   with
                    me plum jam plum jam
06                  (0.5)

07      Rita    :   [hä:,?
                    [hu:,?
                    [hu:,?
                    [
```

```
08    Karin  :  [e:h he he he he .HHH ich ha(h)b heute morgen   den
                [u:h he he he he .HHH i   ha(h)ve today morning the
                [u:h he he he he .HHH this morning i finished the

09    Karin  :  letzten pflaumenmus verspeist. ist     schon    ganz
                last    plum jam     ate.      it is   already completely
                last plum jam. it's quite

10    Karin  :  traurig he he [he he he
                sad he he      [he he he
                sad he he      [he he he
                               [he he he
11    Rita   :                 [kann man den kann man   den auch
                               [can  one it  can  one  it  also
                               [can you can you also

12    Rita   :  schicken,? [(     )
                send,?     [(     )
                mail it,?  [
```

Let us examine Karin's request turn. There are three lexical units which occur prefatory to the request utterance (note that Karin's request utterance consist of a conditional *wenn*-clause and a request): the pronoun *du*, the lexical item *übrigens*, and the expression *weisst du was* (you know what). The lexical item *übrigens* marks the relationship of the current turn to the prior talk. In particular, it marks the turn as an abrupt topical shift and signals that the new turn is sequentially out of place (Egbert 2002, 2003). Note that Karin's request turn is produced after the speakers performed a sequence of possible pre-closing. Schegloff and Sacks (1973: 304) note that after a set of possible pre-closing sequences, speakers may or may not perform the next step which is an exchange of "good-byes". It is, however, in this sequential context that speakers frequently say the unmentioned mentionable item. Put differently, it seems that after performing a set of pre-closings, speakers understand this environment as the last occasion to mention what they did not mention earlier in the talk. It is in this interactional context that Karin produces her request. Note that Karin begins her turn with the pronoun *du* 'you', a summons, and the linguistic expression *weisst du was* 'you know what'. Both function as "attention-getting devices" (Schegloff 1968) by addressing the recipient, Rita, and getting her attention. While the initial turn components do not provide specific information about the type of activity that will be performed by the end of the turn, they do draw the recipients attention to the fact that there will be more talk to come and that it will be specifically for the recipient. Note that in response to Karin's request Rita initiates a non-specified repair displaying some sort of problems with Karin's request turn. Rita's repair may be connected to the disjunctive nature of Karin's request turn (see excerpt 7 in chapter 4 for detailed analysis).

5.4.2   "More specific" prefatory components: Providing some information about the type of activity to come

When a request is occasioned by some items in previous talk, speakers may specifically mention the item that occasioned the new sequence in their new sequence initiation turn. In the next fragment, Thomas begins a new sequence in line 1. Prior to the beginning of this fragment, the two friends talked about Mark's visit to the United States and that Mark plans to bring his camera along since he wants to take many pictures during his trip to the United States. The word *foto* 'picture' seems to have reminded Thomas of a request he has for his friend.

    (5)   Thomas/Mark (Fotos)

```
01->   Thomas :   FOTO     is  a  gutes stichwort genau.    .hh hast du
                  PICTURE  is  a  good   keyword    exactly. .hh have you
                  PICUTRE  is  a  good keyword exactly. .hh do you still

02->   Thomas :   noch   fotos    von  mir mit  langen haarn?
                  still  pictures from me  with long    hair?
                  have any pictures of me with long hair?
```

In line 1, Thomas begins a new request sequence. His pre-request, in lines 1–2, is prefaced by the utterance *foto is a gutes stichwort* 'picture is a good keyword' which indicates the part of the previous talk that reminded him of his request, i.e., the word *foto*. Thomas' turn initial construction displays some concrete relationship between the request and the item in the previous talk which occasioned it. Note also that Thomas produces the adverb *genau* 'exactly' before the pre-request utterance. It seems that the adverb *genau* confirms the fact that Thomas was just being reminded of his request by some item in previous talk. It appears that the adverb *genau* here marks a change in Thomas' epistemological state which was occasioned by his remembering an item.[4] Again, we can see how speakers compose a turn in which they mark an abrupt shift from a previous action and initiate a new action. The prefatory utterance to a pre-request may display some information about the projected new activity. It may, however, not yield a projection of the type of talk that will be followed. In other words, speakers may begin the new sequence with linguistic elements which only mark the initiation of a new sequence and possible topic, but which do not specifically foreshadow the type of projected action.

    The next data fragment is another example of how speakers mark the new request sequence as something that was instantiated by some talk in the preceding turns. This conversation is an excerpt of a conversation between the two sisters, Dora and Carla. Recall that Dora, who is on a student exchange program in the United States, is talking to her sister, Carla, in Germany. Prior to the beginning of this segment, Carla had told her sister about the problems she and her boyfriend had been having with their laptop and that they needed to buy a new one. This topic leads to some other talk about Dora's new laptop which she just recently bought for a relatively low price in the United States. While Dora was talking about the troubles she had with the person from whom she bought the laptop, Carla interrupts her turn and begins a new sequence (line 2). After some prefatory talk, Carla asks her sister whether she could buy her boy friend a laptop in the United States (lines 9–10).

(6)   Dora/Carla (Laptop)

```
01      Dora    :   ich bin ja dann  ganz     zum schl[uß-
                    i    AUX MP then  totally at  en [d-
                    i then totally at the        en [d-
                                                    [
02  -> Carla    :                                  [apropos sach mal
                                                   [by the way tell MP
                                                   [by the way tell me

03  -> Carla    :   was   grad mir einfällt ich weiß ned obs    n  idee
                    what  now  me   remember i   know not if+it  an idea
                    i just remembered i   don't know if it's an

04  -> Carla    :   wä: [r abe:r äh der alex (.) spekuliert im moment
                    we:r[e bu:t uh the alex (.) speculates at moment
                    idea[  bu:t uh alex (.) has also been recently thinking
                        [
05      Dora    :       [mh mh
                       [mh mh
                       [mh mh

06  -> Carla    :   auch  auf n notebook.
                    also  on  a notebook.
                    about a   notebook.

07              :   (.)
08      Dora    :   mhm
                    mhm
                    mhm

09      Carla   :   meinst  du  du  könntest  unter umständen     ihm eins
                    mean+YOU you you could+YOU under circumstances him a
                    do you you think you could possibly buy him

10      Carla   :   besorgen?
                    buy?
                    one?
```

Let us explore Carla's multi-unit turn (lines 2–6) which she produces prefatory to her request. The first unit in her turn *apropos*[5] 'speaking of' is a "misplacement marker" (Schegloff and Sacks 1973). It appears that by initiating her turn with *apropos*, Carla signals that the turn she is initiating is "out of place". Indeed, as we will observe later, her turn initiates a new sequence which is sequentially misplaced. Given that *apropos* means "speaking of x", it seems that the speaker intends to thematically relate two unrelated sequences: the two different actions, i.e., the sequences of a telling and of a request are thematically linked with the linguistic unit *apropos* (both actions have to do with notebooks). With an *apropos* the speaker seems to indicate that while the "topic" (here notebooks) might be the same, the *action type* will be changed, i.e., s/he will not continue the present action but initiate a new one.[6] By utilizing the linguistic expression *apropos* in the turn initial position speakers display some concrete relationship between the upcoming talk and the topic in the previous talk by which it was occasioned.

The second component in her turn *sach mal* 'tell me' is an utterance that addresses the co-participant's attention and projects an action, namely a question. In other words, considering the grammar of the expression *sach mal* we can note that it is an imperative in the second person singular, thereby targeting the co-participant who is asked to perform an action, i.e., a telling. Note that the verb *sach* 'say' is followed by the modal particle *mal*. As was mentioned in chapter 2, German grammar reference textbooks note that the modal/flavoring particle *mal*, which comes from *einmal* 'once/one time', can accompany an imperative; when it does, it softens the request and adds a sense of casualness to the imperative (Engel 1991; Wells 1997; Duden 1998). It seems that the expression *sach mal* projects a question since it does not specifically indicate what the speaker wants his or her co-participant to tell or talk about. So far, these first two units of Cala's turn, that is *apropos* and *sach mal*, project more talk to come. The next component *was grad mir einfällt* 'what I just remembered' indicates that something in the previous talk brought an idea into her mind and that there will be an abrupt shift to a new activity. We can claim that the linguistic expression *was grad mir einfällt* foreshadows subsequent turn(s) and one that is topically related to previous talk. Carla continues by uttering *ich weiss ned obs n idee wär* 'I'm not sure if this would be an idea'. This phrase seems to be doing two things: first, by uttering the word *idee* 'idea' Carla indicates that the talk that will come up will express an idea that she has; additionally, the disclaimer *ich weiss ned* 'I don't know' signals some hedging activity (or insecurity) on Carla's side. In doing so, she allows her sister to project some "delicate" aspect of the subsequent talk. Note that she continues by saying that her boyfriend, Alex, has been thinking about buying a new notebook, to which Dora responds with a continuer. It is in this sequential context that Carla makes her request in line 9. In sum, the exploration of the grammatical construction of Carla's turn reveals how speakers design the first units of their turn to mark the turn as the beginning of a new activity (i.e., a request). Furthermore, we saw that Carla's turn composition also projects that more talk is in progress. In addition, Carla's turn design seems to supply some context in the prefatory talk for the upcoming request turn. In particular, considering the type of request Carla is about to make, it seems that her prefatory talk is preparing her for a delicate matter. Note also another interactional feature of Carla's prefatory talk, namely delaying the dispreferred action of request.

5.4.3   "Specific" prefatory components to request utterances: Providing more information about the type of action projected

Speakers also may use linguistic expressions which both project an upcoming action, and also facilitate foreshadowing the type of action that will come next. In the next data fragment, Carla produces a pre-request in lines 3–6. She and her sister Dora have been talking about their winter plans; at one point in the course of this topic, Dora mentions that skiing would be an activity that they could do. Dora's mentioning of skiing seems to remind Carla to ask her sister whether she, Dora, needed her skates (lines 3–6).

(7)   Dora/Carla (Schlittschuh)

```
01      Dora    : he. he. o::h gott skifahren wäre  was   me   machen
                  he. he. o::h god   skiing    would what we   make
                  he. he. o::h god skiing would be something we

02      Dora    : [können.
                  [could.
                  [could do.
                  [
03 ->   Carla   : [.hhh horch mal ä:h he:: .hh genau    da    kann ich dich
                  [.hhh listen MP u:h he:: .hh exactly there can  i   you
                  [.hhh listen u:h he:: .hh exactly now i can

04 ->   Carla   : mal gleich anbaggern brauchst du   ä:hm, im
                  MP  now    bug        need     you  u:hm, in
                  bug you uh:m, do you need your skates

05 ->   Carla   : wintersemester  wenn du   wieder nüberfliegst deine
                  winter semester when you again  PRX+fly       your
                  in the winter semester when you fly over

06 ->   Carla   : schlittschuh?
                  ice-skates?
                  again?

07              (0.8)
```

```
08 -> Dora    : ä:hm, pfr: .hh kaum     ä:h ne. .hh ä:-ä: [in law-1-
                u:hm, pfr: .hh hardly  u:h no. .hh  u:-u: [in law-1-
                u:hm, pfr: .hh hardly  u:h no. .hh  u:-u:[in law-1-
```

In line 3, Carla begins a new turn in terminal overlap with her sister's turn by producing an audible inbreath and the linguistic expression *horch mal* 'listen'. The phrase *horch mal* appears to function similarly to English phrases such as "hey" or "listen" which normally mark a new-topic-initial turn (Schegloff 1980: 14). In this excerpt, *horch mal* marks the abrupt shift to a new sequence from the previous activity, i.e., doing topic talk. Note that after a couple of speech perturbations and a short inbreath, Carla utters the idiomatic phrase *da kann ich dich mal gleich anbaggern* 'now I can bug you'. Carla's utterance projects that an action will be followed and that it would be directed to Dora. Note furthermore that this phrase occurs just before the pre-request in the same turn, thereby projecting together with the pre-request the next action of request.

5.4.4   "Most-specific" prefatory components to request utterances: Providing the most information about the projected action

An upcoming request may be projected by speakers when composing the beginning of their turn. The next data segment exemplifies such a case. The request sequence happening in this excerpt has already been discussed in chapter 4. Here, however, the focus will be on the utterances prefatory to the request turn. Recall that this is a conversation between Markus, who is on a student exchange program in the United States, and his friend, Klaus, in Germany. The request sequence involves Klaus asking his friend to get him some information about the price of a specific tennis racket (line 5). Prior to the beginning of this excerpt, Markus and Klaus talked about new and old pubs in the college town in which Klaus lives. Klaus claims that things have been quite exciting in the new pubs. In response to this, Markus says that he believes this claim (line 1). It is in this context that Klaus asks Markus to perform a service for him (line 2–3).

(8)   Markus/Klaus (Tennisschläger)

```
01     Markus : ich glaube [das
                i believe  [that
                i believe  [it
                           [
02 ->  Klaus  : ·          [MARKUS genau    das  wollte  ich
                           [MARKUS exactly  that wanted  i
                           [MARKUS exactly  that's what  i
```

```
03 ->  Klaus  : noch  bitten
                still request
                wanted to request


04            (0.2)


05 ->  Klaus  : erkundige dich      ma:l nach  'em tennisschläger.
                inform    yourself MP   after a   tennis racket.
                get some information about a tennis racket.


06            (0.5)


07     Markus : ja=
                yes=
                yes=


08     Klaus  : =und zwar (0.2)  nach   einem wilson prostar
                =and MP   (0.2) after a    wilson prostar
                =about (0.2) a wilson prostar


09     Klaus  : der edberg schläger.
                The edberg racket.
                the edberg racket.


10     Markus : also  ein  moment ich muss  mal aufschreiben da.
                so    a    moment i   must MP  PRXwrite      there.
                just a moment there i have to make a note


11            (0.5)
```

Note that the request sequence in the above data segment does not begin with
Klaus's request turn in line 5. The request sequence actually begins with Klaus's
turn in lines 2–3; a turn type which projects the upcoming action, namely the
request. By explicitly mentioning what he will do in the utterance *das wollt ich
noch bitten* 'that's what I wanted to request', Klaus projects the occurrence of a
turn type in the following turn(s), namely a request. Note that Klaus' turn starts
with a summons, i.e., his friend's name *Markus*, which is followed by the adverb
genau 'exactly'. Considering the sequential placement of the friend's name and
the way Klaus produces the name, it seems that the request has just been brought
to Klaus' mind. Support for this claim can be found in the fact that the summons
begins a new sequence and is produced louder than the surrounding talk. Another
element supporting the claim that the request has just been brought to Klaus'
mind is the adverb *genau* 'exactly'. As was discussed in data fragment 5, the adverb
genau seems to mark a change in a speaker's epistemological state which is occasioned by the speaker's remembering a request. To reiterate, Klaus begins his turn
with a summons, thereby marking his turn as the beginning of a new sequence.
He then continues the turn by announcing that he wanted to request something

from his friend. Klaus' turn design foreshadows the particular type of action which will follow next. Furthermore, it seems that Klaus' action projection turn can be interpreted as preliminary or "prefatory" (Schegloff 1980: 116) to the projected action of request.

5.5.   Discussion

The present chapter focused on two aspects of request sequences in the corpus. One aspect involved the sequential contexts in which the requests were produced. The other aspect had to do with the ways speakers managed to introduce their new activity. The chapter began with a discussion that the activity of requesting may be occasioned by some prior talk, and that speakers employ various interactional strategies to introduce their request sequence. It was noted that similar to topical shifts, request sequences may be introduced into the conversation at a moment that fitted naturally with the previous turn. A related observation was that the pre-request or request turn was topically connected to the previous turn and was thereby gradually introduced into the ongoing conversation. It was also noted that a number of cases of request sequences were initiated rather abruptly into the ongoing conversation. In this context, saying that a request sequence was initiated abruptly means that the turn in which the pre-request or request utterances occurred was topically disconnected from the previous talk.

While describing the sequential contexts in which speakers produced their requests, the analysis also focused on the organization of multi-unit pre-request and request turns, specifically with the grammar of their turn beginnings. The chapter demonstrated how a speaker's turn beginning design may exhibit aspects of the turn's planned shape and type. The discussion illustrated that speakers may utilize specific linguistic components, produced as "prefatory" to the pre-request and request utterances, in order to signal that they are in the process of initiating a new activity which has been occasioned by some prior talk. An investigation of the sequential placement of these linguistic components in combination with their semantic content revealed that they serve a specific interactional function. Four categories of prefatory components to pre-request and request utterances were suggested:

(a) The "non-specific" prefatory components to request utterances. These components occur in turn initial position and mark the request as an item that has just been brought to the speaker's mind. They function as attention-getting devices, and signal the beginning of a new activity while at the same time projecting more talk. They do not, however, reveal any information about the content or type of talk that will follow. Hence, I labeled them the "non-specific" prefatory components.

(b) The "more-specific" prefatory components to request utterances. These components occur in turn initial position; compared to "non-specific" components, they provide more information about what item in the previous talk occasioned the new sequence, thereby displaying some connection to the previous turn and possibly projecting some aspect of the topic of the following action. However, these components do not project the action type that is forthcoming.

(c) The "specific" prefatory components to request utterances. These are components which not only project more talk, but also foreshadow the possible type of action to expect. They do not, however, specifically reveal the type of projected action.

(d) The "most-specific" prefatory components. These are units which exhibit the most specific information about the type of action that they project. In other words, they function as action projections by mentioning the type of action to be expected.

To reiterate, the present chapter illustrated the importance of turn beginnings to the projectability of the turn. It was demonstrated how the turn beginning constructions are the earliest resource for speakers to project the unfolding turn-shape and the type of action that is being performed. The chapter demonstrated the importance of the grammatical structures of a language as one of the fundamental resource for speakers to project the shape of the unfolding turn and its ultimate performed action. Indeed, this feature of allowing the recipient of the current turn to inspect what is "in play" facilitates coordination of social activities in interaction.[7] It can be noted here that the effect of projectability of turns may maximize collaboration and solidarity (Heritage 1984a) in everyday interaction.

Notes

1. The following example which is taken from Drew and Holt (1998: 500) exemplifies how speakers utilize figurative expressions as means to close a topic and move to another activity. The turn in which the speaker produces a figurative expression is marked by arrow 1; the turns in which the recipient briefly agrees with the idiomatic expression is marked by arrow 2, and the turn in which a new topic is shown as arrow 3:

(5) [Field:J86:1:4:6]
     Gwen: You know it wz: so lovely an' everything [y know
     Lesley: [nYe:s.
     Gwen: All character 'n (0.3) beautiful.

Lesley:	Ye:s.
	(0.7)
1 → Gwen:	B't I suppose she must 'v come t' the end of 'er (.) tether 'n just walked out the[n.
2 → Lesley:	[Yes.
	(0.8)
2 → Lesley:	Oh what a shame.
	(.)
2 → Gwen:	Ye:s [it's a shame
3 → Lesley:	[Anywa:y e- so you don't know any mo:re th'n...

2. I would like to thank Andrea Golato for making this data segment available to me.

3. To my knowledge the interactional function of the German speech tokens *ah* (oh) and *ach* (oh) have not been systematically researched. In my collection of request sequences, they seem to function as disjunctive markers which mark the occurrence of the new topic initiation turns as sequentially out of place. The German speech tokens *ah* and *ach* seem also to have a similar function as the English particle "oh" which signals some kind of change in the speaker's current state of knowledge (Heritage 1984b). However, further research is needed to find out in what interactional environments these token occur and whether their usage is interchangeable.

4. It seems that the adverb *genau* may perform a specific interactional function depending on where it is placed in a turn. The analysis of request turn initial components suggests that one particular placement for such a lexical item is in an environment in which an item is brought to the speaker's mind. *Genau* seems to mark an epistemological shift in the speaker's mind, namely remembering an item that he or she wanted to mention earlier. My analysis of *genau* is obviously limited to request sequences. Further research of the interactional function of *genau* in other sequential contexts is needed.

5. *Apropos* is a French loan word (à propos) in the German language which means "übringes" (by the way), "da wir gerade davon sprechen" (talking about/ speaking of) (Duden 1996). The instances of *apropos* in my corpus occupy turn initial position and seem to mark a thematic connection between the current turn and the previous talk. However, I am not aware of any systematic study of this linguistic expression in real-time conversation.

6. Note that unlike *apropos* an *übrigens* (by the way) in turn initial position, as shown in data segment 4, does not mark any topical relationship.

7. One aspect of prefatory components in pre-request and/or request turn that needs further research is the connection between specificity of the prefatory components and speakers' coordination in performing requests. Such a study would need a larger corpus.

CHAPTER 6

Conclusion

The present study provided a micro-analytic description of instances of request sequences in everyday German conversation. In this chapter, I summarize the main findings presented in the previous chapters and discuss the general implication of those findings. I will also discuss some possible directions for future research.

6.1. Summary of the main findings

Using the framework of conversation analysis, the present study systematically analyzed the grammatical construction and sequential placement of turns produced in request sequences. The main goal of the chapters has been to explore the complex interconnectedness between grammar and social interaction by examining how speakers' turn constructions are oriented to the sequential context of performing the social action of request. In other words, I analyzed how the grammatical structure of each turn is shaped by the context of prior talk, and how each turn establishes a context to which the next turn, including its grammatical and syntactical structure, will be oriented. Additionally, the study demonstrated that not only the grammatical construction of turns, but also their temporal placement within the talk is oriented to the sequential context of requesting. In the following, I summarize chapters 2 through 5.

In chapter 2, I first provided a description of the corpus and the methodological framework. The chapter then continued with a discussion of previous studies on requests, their theoretical framework, and findings. I reported that previous studies on requests in German suggest that German speakers frequently formulate their request utterance as a question including a variety of modal or flavoring articles in order to soften and mitigate the degree of the imposition their request may carry. I then argued that due to the nature of their data corpora (i.e., that they represented collections of non-interactional, isolated sentences), these studies have failed to provide a systematic analysis of the sequential context of requests. More specifically, these studies have failed to demonstrate that the grammatical construction of speakers' utterances is shaped by the sequential context within which they are produced. Therefore, in this chapter, I suggested using conversation analysis as an alternative methodology for exploring the social situation of requests, namely by exploring both the speakers' and the recipients' real-time orientation to the "dispreferred" nature of requests in talk-in-interaction.

In Chapter 3, I closely examined instances of requests in German talk-in-interaction to demonstrate the ways in which utterances accomplished particular actions by virtue of their placement within larger sequences of actions. The chapter began with an illustration of the sequential context in which speakers' turns were interpreted by their recipients as pre-requests, and how recipients' relevant next turns exhibited this reading. The exploration of the linguistic composition of pre-request turns and their sequential placement within the talk suggested three pre-request turn formats. It was shown that pre-request turns may be designed as a question that explores the possibility of a projected request being granted. This pre-request turn format has also been observed in American English data (Levinson 1983; Sacks 1996; Schegloff in press). Another pre-request turn format noted in the corpus was in the form of giving accounts. It was demonstrated that speakers interpreted their co-participant's account for an action or lack of access to an object as a pre-request, and in return offered the object that their co-participant had no access to. The analysis of pre-request turn formats also illustrated that a speaker's mentioning of what they like was understood by their co-participant as a pre-request which subsequently received an offer of the object or service for which they expressed a liking. It was illustrated how speakers utilize these turn-formats as an interactional device to project the action of making a request.

In the second half of the chapter, I examined request sequences in which speakers chose to issue a request, even though the pre-request expansion revealed contingencies on the request compliance. In such situations, I showed that speakers' request turn shapes revealed their orientation towards the contingencies mentioned earlier in the talk by their co-participants. I named these types of requests "contingent requests". The goal of the analysis of such requests was to show ways that speakers employ grammatical and syntactical forms of the language as resources to coordinate the production of the social action of requests, and to manage affiliative work when engaged in performing such a dispreferred social activity. A close examination of instances of contingent requests demonstrated that the production of requests and their turn shapes is closely connected to the local context and the speakers' contributions. More specifically, it was shown that the grammatical structure of contingent request turns exhibited the speaker's understanding of the sequential connection between the prior turn and the activities being managed in previous turns. It was also shown that the majority of contingent requests in the collection contained a conditional *wenn*-clause 'if-clause'. The *wenn*-clauses in such request instances were basically the linguistic realization of the contingent circumstances which were mentioned by their co-participant in the prior talk. Here, I argued that speakers display an orientation to their co-participant at the syntactic as well as the thematic level by incorporating elements from their recipient's prior turn into their conditional *wenn*-clause. In addition to the composition of the *wenn*-clauses, the analysis also focused on their sequential placement within request sequences. It was demonstrated that the position of the *wenn*-clause within the request sequence is tightly connected to preference organization. More specifically, it was noted that by inserting the *wenn*-clause in the initial or mid position of the request turn, speakers delayed the delivery of the object or service they wished to request. I argued that this particular positioning of conditional *wenn*-clauses in the request turn served to display speakers' affiliation with their co-participants, and thereby can be interpreted as supportive of "social solidarity" (Heritage 1984a).

The analysis presented in Chapter 4 paid particular attention to the ways speakers use grammar and syntax as interactional resources to manage affiliative and remedial work when performing a request. Overall, the analysis in this chapter suggested that similar to English conversations, accounts in German are a design feature of requests. A further investigation of the content of accounts for requests suggested that they share a particular design, namely that they commonly addressed "no fault" (Heritage, 1984) issues. In other words, the content expressed in the account for request utterances referred to some "uncontrollable" issue and/or "lack of access" to the requested object. I argued that the "no fault" quality of accounts for requests and the provided background information in the account utterances served to avoid threatening the co-participant's "face" (Goffman 1955) and the social relationship with co-participants, thus maintaining social solidarity (Heritage 1984a).

A close examination of the sequential placements of accounts for requests suggested that accounts occur in different temporal placements within request sequences, and that their different placements perform different interactional functions. Two temporal placements for accounts in request sequences were identified. I showed examples in which speakers built their account into their request turns both immediately following the request utterance, and before a responsive action from their co-participant. I termed this particular placement of accounts in request sequences the "before-request-response" position. I also discussed other instances of the before-request-response position in which an account for a request was provided, specifically in the context of a response which was rather hesitant and in which a possible disagreement with the request was thus projectable. The account was provided before the recipient's response to the request. Considering the before-request-response positions, I noted that these particular placements of accounts are related to preference organization. More specifically, I argued that by placing their accounts for request in such an early position, speakers pursue a preferred responsive action from their co-participant.

In addition to the before-request-response position of accounts, the analysis of temporal placements of accounts in request sequences revealed that speakers also provided an explanation for their request after their co-participant agreed to comply with their request. This particular position was referred to as "after-request-acceptance". I argued that compared to before-request-response positioned accounts, accounts in after-request-acceptance position perform more "remedial work" (Goffman 1971). Put differently, I noted that accounts which occur after the recipient had agreed to comply with the request address repairing the damage the dispreferred action may have caused to the recipient's face, and thereby function as a "threat-and-conflict avoidance" (Heritage 1984a) strategy.

An analysis of German accounts for requests with respect to their grammatical structure also pinpointed some syntactical features of German grammar that can be involved in displaying affiliative moves. It was illustrated that accounts for requests were frequently introduced by the causal connector *weil* displaying a marked word order (in this instance, main clause word order). My discussion of marked word order *weil*-clauses in request sequences in German talk-in-interaction had a two-fold purpose: it served to provide additional examples of the employment of such clauses in spoken German, and to further specify the interactional function such a marked word order may have. I agreed with previous studies of these *weil*-clauses that due to their marked word order, they may be interpretable as separate independent clauses with their own illocutionary force, and that they mitigate the face threatening act of requests (Günthner 1996). In addition, I argued that the earlier placement of the finite verb in accounts for request utterances may be understood as an affiliative move in two ways. First, it was demonstrated that the early placement of the finite verb has to do with account turn cohesion: by placing the verb in the second position, speakers may make a rather elaborative account turn more cohesive for their co-participants. Additionally, I argued that an early placement of the finite verb in an account utterance marked by the causal connector *weil* can accelerate the occurrence of the finite verb which carries the core semantic meaning of the account utterance. Furthermore, I argued that the causal connector *weil* and the second-position of the finite verb provide co-participants with resources for anticipating both what kind of action is under construction, and what it will take to be completed. Overall, my analysis in Chapter 4 suggests that the sequential placement, content and grammatical structure of accounts for requests in German conversation are organized by the underlying structure of social interaction, i.e., by the management of self- and other relationships and the maintenance of social solidarity.

Finally, in chapter 5, I explored yet another aspect of request sequences in German conversation. The chapter focused on the talk that occurred prefatory to pre-request or request utterances at turn beginnings. The examination of pre-request and request turn beginnings illustrated that speakers employed various linguistic units as special interactional devices to mark their request sequence as a new activity, thereby allowing their co-participant to not only project what action is being performed at the moment, but also the type of action(s) which is to be followed. Focusing on the sequential contexts in which pre-request and/or request turns were produced in the corpus and the ways speakers managed to introduce their new activity of request, the analysis showed that grammatical structures of a language serve as one of the fundamental resources for speakers to project the shape of the unfolding turn and its ultimate performed action (Hayashi 2004; Sacks, et al. 1974; Schegloff and Sacks 1973; Streeck 1995; Schegloff 1996). The analysis of the sequential context in which the request sequences were produced suggested that request sequences can be introduced into the conversation gradually, by topically connecting the pre-request or request turn to the previous turn. The analysis also showed that request sequences were also introduced rather abruptly into the ongoing conversation, with no cohesive connection between the current pre-request and request turns with the prior turn.

The investigation of the pre-request and request turn beginnings showed how speakers' turn beginning designs may exhibit aspects of their turn's planned shape and type. The discussion illustrated that speakers may utilize specific linguistic components that are produced as "prefatory" to the pre-request and request utterances in order to signal that they are in the process of initiating a new activity which has been occasioned by some prior talk. Four categories of prefatory components to pre-request and request utterances were suggested in terms of the specific information they indicate. These different types of prefatory components share one specific interactional function: they all signal the beginning of a new activity and, at the same time, project subsequent talk. These categories range from the most "non-specific" prefatory components to request utterances, to the "most-specific" prefatory components. The "non-specific" prefatory components, as their label indicates, do not reveal any information about the type of activity they project. The "most-specific" prefatory components, on the other hand, reveal the most specific information about the type of activity that is to come.

My analysis of prefatory components to pre-request and request utterances demonstrated how the turn beginning constructions are the earliest resource for speakers to use in projecting the unfolding turn-shape and the type of action that is being performed. I argued that allowing the recipient of the current turn to inspect what is "in play" facilitates coordination of social activities in interaction and that the effect of projectability of turns may maximize collaboration and solidarity (Heritage 1984a) in everyday interaction.

6.2. Implications

The major focus of the present study has been to explore the interplay between grammatical construction and the organization of social interaction. In the following section, I discuss some broader implications which the findings presented in the previous chapters suggest.

Overall, the present study offered a descriptive micro-analysis of request sequences within the larger social interaction. The analysis presented in this book differs from previous studies on requests in that it explores requests in their sequential context and thereby demonstrates how, in combination with their linguistic composition, the sequential placement of turns at talk is closely connected to the local context and speakers' contributions. For example, the discussion of pre-request turns in chapter 3 has shown how speakers' utterances are understood by their recipients as pre-requests by virtue of their sequential placement within sequences of actions. Furthermore, the analysis of different temporal placements of *wenn*-clauses and *weil*-clauses within request sequences and the different interactional functions they perform provided evidence that not only the design of actions contributes to the maintenance of social solidarity (Heritage 1984a: 265), but also their sequential placement within the context of the action performed is related to management of affiliative and remedial work.

One major theme in the analysis of request sequences in the corpus was the impact the request activity context has on the grammatical construction of speakers' utterances. The discussions of *wenn*-clauses in chapter 3 and *weil*-clauses in chapter 4 have demonstrated that the grammatical construction of utterances is sensitive to the local management of accomplishing the social action of request. In particular, the analysis of syntactical structure of *weil*-clauses in chapter 4 showed that they all displayed the marked word order (finite verb in the second position), a syntactical structure which has been considered by German standard reference grammars not only as ungrammatical but also a sign of sloppiness when used in the spoken language (Duden 1998; Eisenberg 1999; Engel 1991; Wahrig 2003; Wells 1997). However, as the discussion in chapter 4 showed, this particular grammatical structure cannot be described as incorrect. It was demonstrated that the marked syntactical structure of *weil*-clauses in request sequences serves indeed a very specific interactional function. It was argued that the early placement of the finite verb facilitates overall turn cohesion and projectability. Therefore, this particular grammatical construction of *weil*-clause in request sequences made an additional contribution to the understanding of grammar as a phenomenon which is tightly intertwined with social interaction (Schegloff et al. 1996). In addition, the analysis of *weil*-clauses presented in chapter 4 provided further evidence for the argument that the marked word order of *weil*-clauses is not incorrect but that it is a feature of spoken discourse which serves a particular interactional function (Günthner 1993; Scheutze 2001; Uhmann 1998).

One area to which the findings presented in this book is relevant is language pedagogy. In recent years, there has been the tendency among language and foreign language professionals to recognize the importance of teaching grammar that is derived from empirical studies on real-time conversation rather than idealized sentence-level description (Barraja-Rohan 1997; Celce-Murcia and Larsen-Freeman 1983; Celce-Murcia 1990; Huth 2005; Taleghani-Nikazm 1999). The present study provided a description of how German speakers grammatically compose their utterances when involved in the social action of requesting. In particular, the discussions of grammatical construction and temporal placement of *wenn*-clauses and *weil*-clauses, and the analysis of turn beginning components such as *horch mal, sach mal, apropos, foto ist ein gutes Stichwort* among others, provide an empirically grounded discussion of German grammar from a language *in situ* perspective. Additionally, the findings of the present study make a contribution to the field of teaching German as a foreign/second language, especially as concerns foreign language textbook design. It has been noted that dialogues in textbooks do not follow patterns of naturally occurring talk and fail to introduce and/or teach speakers' verbal behavior in their sequential context (Han 1992; Huth 2005; Scott 1987; Scotton and Bernstein 1988; Taleghani-Nikazm 1999; Wong 2002). Studies on how speakers manage a particular social action may serve as a valuable source for teachers and textbook designers who wish to incorporate authentic target language dialogues into their pedagogical materials.

And finally, the findings presented in this book make a particularly strong contribution to the growing body of research on German talk-in-interaction which explores the relationship between the organization of grammar and the organization of social interaction (Auer and Uhmann 1982; Auer 1993, 2000; Gohl 2000a, 2000b; Golato 2002a, 2002b, 2005; Günthner 1993; Uhmann, 1998; Selting and Couper-Kuhlen 2001; Scheutz 2001).

6.3. Avenues for future research

The findings in this book are based on data collected from everyday conversations among adult friends and family. As was mentioned in chapter 2, the corpus for this study is rather limited in scope, since the majority of the collected instances of requests came from audio-recorded telephone conversations which exhibited rather complex request sequences (this was possibly due to the nature of the requested object or service). Therefore, it would only make sense to expand the corpus to include additional instances of request sequences which occurred in face-to-face interactions. Another suggestion to expand the scope of the corpus would be to include other kinds of interactions, such as child-adult and child-child interactions. As has been found with English, the present study of the organization of requests in German conversations among adults showed a similar preference for offers over requests. This preference was demonstrated in the occurrence of pre-request sequences in the corpus. It would be interesting to examine the preference organization of requests in child-adult interactions. As far as I am aware, there has been only one empirical study on requests in child-adult English conversation. While Wootton's (1981) study of the organization of requests in the "asymmetric power balance" of child-parent interaction offers us some significant insights on parents' responsive behavior when receiving a request from their child, the analysis is limited to granting and rejecting requests by parents and does not include an analysis of interactional moves a child makes when performing a request. Therefore, further systematic research on the preference organization of requests in child-adult and child-child interaction is necessary. Such a study may expand our understanding of child language acquisition and socialization (Ochs 1988) by exploring ways the underlying social organization of making requests impacts the design of request utterances produced by children.

An additional setting that would expand the corpus for the study of request sequences is the institutional setting, in particular the foreign/second language classroom. Considering the two different speech exchange systems of "unequal power" (teacher-student) and "equal power" (student-student) (Markee 2000) in classrooms, an investigation of preference organization of requests in classroom interaction may shed light on our understanding of second language acquisition. In particular, an analysis of how learners deploy learned grammar and syntax as resources to construct turns at talk in order to accomplish the action of request may reveal information about students' communicative competence (Canale and Swain 1980; Hymes 1972). Furthermore, such findings about learners' language development might help professionals in the field with facilitating language acquisition. In addition to classroom interaction, a study of request sequences in talk at work might provide us with information about how pre-request and request turns are impacted by the institutional context and, conversely, how the context of a particular setting such as the workplace organizes turn composition in request sequences.

Another direction for further research might be to examine the function of the adverb *genau* 'exactly' in German talk-in-interaction. The discussion of prefatory components to pre-request and request utterances in chapter 5 pointed out that the adverb *genau* in turn beginnings had a specific interactional function in the context of beginning the new activity of requesting. A glance through my German data transcripts suggests that the lexical item of *genau* also occurs in other interactional environments than the context of request sequences. Therefore, further systematic research on the interactional function of *genau* in everyday German talk-in-interaction seems necessary. Such research might advance our understanding of German grammar in interaction. Yet another direction for further research might be to examine the placement and function of the tokens *ach* 'oh' and *ah* 'oh' which occur frequently in turn initial positions. While the interactional function of English token *oh* has been researched extensively (Heritage 1984b; 2002), to my knowledge there has been no systematic study conducted on the sequential aspects of the German tokens *ach* and *oh*. Finally, when conducted with reference to the work on grammar and social interaction in English (Ford 1993; Ochs et al. 1996; Sacks et al. 1974; Selting and Couper-Kuhlen 2001), any of the above suggested directions for further research on German talk-in-interaction will advance our understanding of the reflexive relationship between grammar and social interaction, in particular, between the structure of the German language and German social organization.

References

Antaki, C. (1994). *Explaining and Arguing: Social Organization of Accounts*. London, Thousand Oaks, New Delhi: Sage Publications.

Atkinson, J. M., & Heritage, J. (Eds.). (1984). *Structures of Social Action. Studies in Conversation Analysis*. Cambridge: Cambridge University Press.

Auer, P. (1993). Zur Verbspitzenstellung im gesprochenen Deutsch [The verb in first position in spoken German]. *Deutsche Sprache, 3*, 193–222.

Auer, P. (2000). Pre-and post positioning of *wenn*-clauses in spoken and written German. In E. a. B. K. Couper-Kuhlen (Ed.), *Cause-Condition-Concession-Contrast: Cognitive and Discourse Perspectives* (pp. 173–204). Berlin: Mouton de Gruyter.

Auer, P. (2005). Projection in Interaction and Projection in Grammar. *Text, 25(1), 7–36, 25(1)*, 7–36.

Auer, P. J. C., & Uhmann, S. (1982). Aspekte der konversationellen Organisation von Bewertungen [Aspects of the conversational organisation of assessments]. *Deutsche Sprache, 10*, 1–32.

Barraja-Rohan, A.-M. (1997). Teaching conversation and sociocultural norms with conversation analysis. In A. J. Liddicoat & C. Crozet (Eds.), *Teaching language, teaching culture* (Vol. 14, pp. 71–88). Australia.

Blum-Kulka, S. (1987). Indirectness and politeness in requests: same or different? *Journal of Pragmatics, 11*, 134–146.

Blum-Kulka, S., House, J., & Kasper, G. (Eds.). (1989). *Cross-cultural pragmatics: requests and apologies* (Vol. XXXI). Norwood, New Jersey: Ablex Publishing Corporation.

Blum-Kulka, S., & Olshtain, E. (1984). Requests and apologies: A cross-cultural study of speech act realization patterns (CCSARP). *Applied Linguistics, 5(3)*, 196–213.

Brown, P., & Levinson, S. (1978). Universals in language usage: politeness phenomena. In E. Goody (Ed.), *Questions and Politeness* (pp. 56–289). Cambridge: Cambridge University Press.

Brown, P., & Levinson, S. (1987). *Politeness*. Cambridge: Cambridge University Press.

Canale, M., & Swain, M. (1980). Theoretical bases of communicative approaches to second language teaching and testing. *Applied Linguistics, 1*, 1–47.

Celce-Murcia, M. (1990). Discourse analysis and grammar instruction. *Annual Review of Applied Linguistics, 11*, 135–151.

Celce-Murcia, M., & Larsen-Freeman, D. (1983). *The grammar book: an ESL/EFL teacher's course*. Rowley, MA: Newbury House.

Cody, M. J., & McLaughlin, M. L. (1990). Interpersonal accounting. In H. Giles & W. P. Robinson (Eds.), *The Handbook of Language and Social Psychology*. Chichester: Wiley.

Couper-Kuhlen, E. (1999). Coherent voicing: On prosody in conversational reported speech. In W. Bublitz & U. Lenk (Eds.), *Coherence in Spoken and Written Discourse* (pp. 11–33). Amsterdam and Philadelphia: Benjamins.

Dancygier, B. (1993). Interpreting conditionals: Time, knowledge, and causation. *Journal of Pragmatics, 19*, 403–434.

Dancygier, B., & Sweetser, E. (1996). Conditionals, distancing, and alternative spaces. In A. E. Goldberg (Ed.), *Conceptual structure, discourse and language* (pp. 83–98). Stanford: CSLI Publications.

Dancygier, B., & Sweetser, E. (2000). Constructions with *if, since,* and *because*: Causality, epistemic stance, and clause order. In E. a. B. K. Couper-Kuhlen (Ed.), *Cause-Condition-Concession-Contrast* (pp. 111–142). Berlin: Mouton de Gruyter.

Davidson, J. (1984). Subsequent versions of invitations, offers, requests, and proposals dealing with potential or actual rejection. In J. M. Atkinson & J. Heritage (Eds.), *Structures of Social Action. Studies in Conversation Analysis* (pp. 102–128). Cambridge: Cambridge University Press.

Draper, S. (1988). What's going on in everyday explanation? In C. Antaki (Ed.), *Analysing everyday explanation.* London: Sage.

Drew, P. (1997). "Open" class repair initiators in response to sequential sources of troubles in conversation. *Journal of Pragmatics, 28,* 69–101.

Drew, P. a. H., Elizabeth. (1998). Figures of speech: idiomatic expressions and the management of topic transition in conversation. *Language in Society, 27,* 495–522.

Duden: Grammatik der deutschen Gegenwartssprache. (6 ed. Vol. 4)(1998). 6 ed. Vol. 4). Mannheim: Dudenverlag.

Egbert, M. (1996). Context-sensitivity in conversation: Eye gaze and the German repair initiator 'bitte'? *Language in Society, 25*(4), 587–612.

Egbert, M. (1997). Some interactional achievements of other-initiated repair in multiperson conversation. *Journal of Pragmatics, 27,* 611–634.

Egbert, M. (2002). Syntaktische Merkmale von übrigens in seiner Hauptposition: Im Mittelfeld des Verb-Zweit-Satzes [Syntactical characteristics of übrigens 'by the way' in its main position: In the middle field of verb-second-sentences]. *Zeitschrift fuer Germanistische Linguistik, 30*(1), 1–22.

Egbert, M. (2003). Die interaktionelle Relevanz einer gemeinsamen Vorgeschichte: Zur Bedeutung und Funktion von übrigens in deutschen Alltagsgesprächen [The interactional relevancy of joint pre-story: On the meaning and function of übrigens 'by the way' in everyday German]. *Zeitschrift fuer Sprachwissenschaft, 22*(2), 189–212.

Eisenberg, P. (1989). *Grundriß der deutschen Grammatik [Outline of the German grammar]* (2nd rev. ed.). Stuttgart: J.B. Metzlersche Verlagsbuchhandlung.

Engel, U. (1991). *Deutsche Grammatik [German Grammar].* Heidelberg: Julius Gross Verlag.

Eslamirasekh, Z. (1993). A Cross-Cultural Comparison of the Requestive Speech Act Realization Patterns in Persian and American English. *Pragmatics and Language Learning, 4,* 85–101.

Ford, C. E. (1993). *Grammar in Interaction: Adverbial Clauses in American English Conversations.* Cambridge and New York: Cambridge University Press.

Ford, C. E. (1994). Dialogic aspects of talk and writing: *because* on the interactive-edited continuum. *Text, 14*(4), 531–554.

Ford, C. E. (1997). Speaking conditionally: Some contexts for *if*-clauses in conversation. In A. A. a. R. Dirven (Ed.), *On Conditionals Again* (pp. 387–413). Amsterdam/Philadelphia: John Benjamins Publishing Company.

Ford, C. E., Fox, B. A., & Thompson, S. A. (Eds.). (2002). *The Language of Turn and Sequence.* New York: Oxford University Press.

Ford, C. E., & Mori, J. (1991). Causal markers in Japanese and English conversations: a cross-linguistic study of interactional grammar. *Pragmatics, 4*(1), 31–61.

Ford, C. E., & Mori, J. (1994). Causal markers in Japanese and English conversations: a cross-linguistic study of interactional grammar. *Pragmatics, 4*(1), 31–61.

Ford, C. E., & Thompson, S. A. (1986). Conditionals in discourse: A text-based study from

English. In A. t. M. Elizabeth Closs Traugott, Judy Snitzer Reilly and Charles A. Ferguson (Ed.), *On Conditionals* (pp. 353–373). Cambridge: Cambridge University Press.

Ford, C. E., & Thompson, S. A. (1996). Interactional units in conversation: Syntactic, intonational and pragmatic resources for the management of turns. In E. Ochs, E. A. Schegloff & S. A. Thompson (Eds.), *Interaction and Grammar* (pp. 134–184). Cambridge: Cambridge University Press.

Fox, B. A. (Ed.). (1996). *Studies in Anaphora*. Amsterdam/Philadelphia: John Benjamins.

Fox, B. A., Hayashi, M., & Jasperson, R. (1996). Resources and repair: A cross-linguistic study of syntax and repair. In E. Ochs, E. A. Schegloff & S. A. Thompson (Eds.), *Interaction and Grammar* (pp. 185–237). Cambridge: Cambrdige University Press.

Fukushima, S. (1996). Request strategies in British English and Japanese. *Language Sciences, 18*(3–4), 671–688.

Garcia, C. (1993). Making a request and responding to it: A case study of Peruvian Spanish speakers. *Journal of Pragmatics, 19*, 127–152.

Goffman, E. (1955). On Face-Work: An Analysis of Ritual Elements in Social Interaction. *Psychiatry, 18*, 213–231.

Goffman, E. (1971). *Relations in Public. Microstudies of the Public Order*. New York: Basic Books.

Gohl, C. (2000a). Causal relations in spoken discourse: Asyndetic constructions as a means for giving reasons. In E. Couper-Kuhlen & B. Kortmann (Eds.), *Cause, condition, concession, contrast: Cognitive and discourse perspectives* (pp. 83–111). Berlin: Mouton De Gruyter.

Gohl, C. (2000b). Zwischen Kausalität und Konditionalität: Begründende wenn-Konstruktionen [Between causality and conditionality: Causal wenn 'if'-construction]. *InLiSt (Interaction and Linguistic Structures), 24*, 33.

Golato, A. (2000). An innovative German quotative for reporting on embodied actions: *Und ich so/und er so* 'and I'm like/and he's like'. *Journal of Pragmatics, 32*, 29–54.

Golato, A. (2002a). German compliment responses. *Journal of Pragmatics, 34*, 547–571.

Golato, A. (2002b). Grammar and interaction: Reported discourse and subjunctive in German. *Zeitschrift fuer Germanistische Linguistik, 22*(1), 24–55.

Golato, A. (2002c). Self-quotation in German: Reporting on past decisions. In T. a. R. Güldemann, M. V. (Ed.), *Reported Discourse: A Meeting Ground for Different Linguistic Domains* (pp. 49–70). Amsterdam/Philadelphia: John Benjamins.

Golato, A. (2003). Studying compliment responses: A comparison of DCTs and recordings of naturally occurring talk. *Applied Linguistics, 24*(1), 90–121.

Golato, A. (2005). *Compliments and Compliment Resoponses: Grammatical structure and sequential organization*. Amsterdam/Philadelphia: John Benjamins.

Goldberg, J. A. (1978). Amplitude shift. A mechanism for the affiliation of utterances in coversational interaction. In J. N. Schenkein (Ed.), *Studies in the organization of conversation interaction* (pp. 199–218). New York: Academic Press.

Goodwin, C. (1979). The interactive construction of a sentence in natural conversation. In G. Psathas (Ed.), *Everyday Language: Studies in Ethnomethodology* (pp. 97–121). New York: Irvington Publishers.

Goodwin, C. (1980). Restarts, pauses, and the achievement of a state of mutual gaze at turn beginning. *Sociological Inquiry, 50*(3–4), 272–302.

Goodwin, C. (1981). *Conversational Organization. Interaction between Speakers and Hearers*. New York: Academic Press.

Goodwin, C. (1996). Transparent vision. In E. Ochs, E. A. Schegloff & S. A. Thompson (Eds.), *Interaction and Grammar* (pp. 370–404). Cambridge: Cambridge University Press.

Goodwin, C., & Heritage, J. (1990). Conversation Analysis. *Annual Review of Anthropology, 19,* 283–307.

Günthner, S. (1993). weil- man kann es ja wissenschaftlich untersuchen - Diskurspragmatische Aspekte der Wortstellung in WEIL-Sätzen [Because-one can study it scientifically-discourse pragmatic aspects of word order in weil 'because'-clauses]. *Linguistische Berichte, 143,* 37–59.

Günthner, S. (1996). From Subordination to Coordination? Verb-Second Position in German Clausal and Concessive Constructions. *Pragmatics, 6*(3), 323–356.

Günthner, S. (1999a). Polyphony and the 'layering of voices' in reported dialogues: An analysis of the use of prosodic devices in everyday reported speech. *Journal of Pragmatics, 31,* 685–708.

Günthner, S. (1999b). Wenn-Sätze im Vor-Vorfeld: Ihre Formen und Funktionen in der gesprochenen Sprache [Wenn 'if'-clauses in pre-prefield: Their forms and functions in the spoken language]. *InLiSt (Interaction and Linguistic Structures), 11,* 34.

Han, C.-h. (1992). A comparative study of compliment responses: Korean females in Korean interactions and in English interactions. *Working Papers in Educational Linguistics, 8*(2), 17–31.

Harren, I. (2001). "Ne?" in Alltagsgesprächen-Interaktive Funktionen und Positionierung in Turn und Sequenz. Unpublished M.A. Thesis, Universität Oldenburg, Oldenburg.

Hayashi, M. (1997). An exploration of Sentence-Final Uses of the Quotative Particle in Japanese Spoken Discourse. In H.-m. Sohn & J. Haig (Eds.), *Japanese/Korean Linguistics* (Vol. 6, pp. 565–581). Stanford: Center Study Language & Information.

Hayashi, M. (1999). When grammar and interaction meet: A study of co-participant completion in Japanese conversation. *Human Studies, 22,* 475–499.

Hayashi, M. (2003). *Joint Utterance Construction in Japanese Conversation.* Amsterdam/Philadelphia: John Benjamins.

Hayashi, M. (2004). Projection and grammar: notes on the "action-projecting" use of the distal demonstrative *are* in Japanese. *Journal of Pragmatics, 36,* 1337–1374.

Hayashi, M. (1994). A comparative study of self-repair in English and Japanese conversation. In N. Akatsuka (Ed.), *Japanese/Korean Linguistics* (Vol. 4, pp. 77–93). Stanford: CSLI Publications.

Hayashi, M., Mori, J., & Takagi, T. (2002). Contingent achievement of co-tellership in a Japanese conversation: An analysis of talk, gaze, and gesture. In C. E. Ford, B. A. Fox & S. A. Thompson (Eds.), *The Language of Turn and Sequence* (pp. 81–122). Oxford: Oxford University Press.

Heritage, J. (1984a). *Garfinkel and Ethnomethodology.* Cambridge: Polity Press, in association with Basil Blackwell, Oxford.

Heritage, J. (1984b). A change-of-state token and aspects of its sequential placement. In J. M. Atkinson & J. Heritage (Eds.), *Structures of social action. Studies in conversation analysis* (pp. 299–345). Cambridge: Cambridge University Press.

Heritage, J. (1985). Analyzing news interviews: aspects of the production of talk for an over-hearing audience. In V. Dijk (Ed.), *Handbook of Discourse Analysis* (Vol. 3, pp. 95–117). London: Academic Press.

Heritage, J. (1988). Explanations as accounts: a conversation analytic perspective. In C. Antaki (Ed.), *Analalyzing Everyday Explanation: a Casebook of Methods* (pp. 127–144). Sage.

Heritage, J. (2002). *Oh*-prefaced responses to assessments: A method of modifying agreement/disagreement. In C. E. Ford, B. A. Fox & S. A. Thompson (Eds.), *The language of turn and sequence* (pp. 196–224). Oxford: Oxford University Press.

House, J. (Ed.). (1989). *Politeness in English and German: The functions of please and bitte*. Norwood: Ablex Publishing Corp.

House, J., & Kasper, G. (1981). Politeness markers in English and German. In F. Coulmas (Ed.), *Conversational Routine. Explorations in Standardized Communication Situations and Prepatterned Speech* (Vol. 2, pp. 157–185). The Hague, Paris, New York: Mouton Publishers.

Hutchby, I., & Wooffitt, R. (1998). *Conversation Analysis. Principles, Practices and Application*. Cambridge: Polity Press.

Huth, T. (2005). *Talking perspective: Conversation analysis and culture in the German foreign language classroom*. Unpublished Doctoral Dissertation, The University of Kansas.

Hymes, D. H. (1972). On communicative competence. In J. B. Pride & J. Holmes (Eds.), *Sociolinguistics* (pp. 269–293). Harmondsworth: Penguin.

Jefferson, G. (1980). The abominable *Ne?* An Exploration of post-response pursuit of response. In P. Schröder & H. Steger (Eds.), *Dialogforschung. Jahrbuch 1980 des Instituts für deutsche Sprache* (pp. 53–88). Düsseldorf: Pädagogischer Verlag Schwann.

Jefferson, G. (1984a). Transcription notation. In J. M. Atkinson & J. Heritage (Eds.), *Structures of social action* (pp. ix-xvi). Cambridge: Cambridge University Press.

Jefferson, G. (1984b). On stepwise transition from talk about a trouble to inappropriately next-positioned matters. In J. M. Atkinson & J. Heritage (Eds.), *Structures of Social Action. Studies in Conversation Analysis* (pp. 191–222). Cambridge: Cambridge University Press.

Keller, R. (1995). The epistemic weil. In D. Stein & S. Wright (Eds.), *Subjectivity and Subjectivisation: Linguistic Perspectives* (pp. 16–30). Cambridge: Cambridge University Press.

Koike, D. (1989). Requests and the role of deixis in politeness. *Journal of Pragmatics, 13*(2), 187–202.

Koike, D. (1994). Negation in Spanish and English suggestions and requests: mitigating effects? *Journal of Pragmatics, 21*, 513–526.

Koshik, I. (2005). *Beyon Rhetorical Questions: Assertive questions in everyday interaction*. Amsterdam/Philadelphia: John Benjamins.

Küper, C. (1984). Zum sprechaktbezogenen Gebrauch der Kausalverknüpfer denn und weil: Grammatische-pragmatische Interrelationen. [On Speech-Act-Related Usage of the Causal Conjunctions denn and weil: Grammatical-Pragmatic Interrelations.]. *Linguistische Berichte, 92*(August), 15–30.

Küper, C. (1991). Geht die Nebensatzstellung im Deutschen verloren? Zur pragmatischen Funktion der Wortstellung in Haupt- und Nebensätzen. [Is Subordinate Clause Order Being Lost in German? On the Pragmatic Function of Word Order in Main and Subordinate Clauses.]. *1991, 19*(2), 133–158.

le Pair, R. (1996). Spanish request strategies: a cross-cultural analysis from an intercultural perspective. *Language Sciences, 18*(3–4), 651–670.

Leech, G. N. (1983). *Principles of pragmatics*. London: Longman.

Lerner, G. H. (1987). Collaborative Turn Sequences: Sentence Construction and Social Action: (The University of California, Irvine).

Lerner, G. H. (1991). On the syntax of sentences-in-progress. *Language in Society, 20*, 441–458.

Lerner, G. H. (1993). Collectivities in action: establishing the relevance of conjoined participation in conversation. *Text, 13,* 213–245.

Lerner, G. H. (1996a). Finding "face" in the preference structures of talk-in-interaction". *Social Psychology Quarterly, 59*(4), 303–321.

Lerner, G. H. (1996b). On the 'semi-permeable' character of grammatical units in conversation: conditional entry into the turn space of another speaker. In E. Ochs, S. Thompson & E. A. Schegloff (Eds.), *Grammar and Interaction* (pp.?).

Lerner, G. H. (2002). Turn-sharing: The choral co-production of talk-in-interaction. In C. E. Ford, B. A. Fox & S. A. Thompson (Eds.), *The Language of Turn and Sequence* (pp. 225–256). Oxford: Oxford University Press.

Lerner, G. H. (2004). On the place of linguistic resources in the organization of turn-in-interaction: Grammar as action in prompting a speaker to elaborate. *Research on Language and Social Interaction, 37*(2), 151–185.

Levinson, S. (1983). *Pragmatics.* Cambridge: Cambridge University Press.

Markee, N. (2000). *Conversation Analysis.* Mahwah, New Jersey: Lawrence Erlbaum Associates, Publishers.

Marquez Reiter, R. (2000). *Linguistic Politeness in Britain and Uruguay.* Amsterdam/Philadelphia: John Benjamins.

Maynard, D. W. (1980). Placement of topic changes in conversation. *Semiotica, 30*(3/4), 263–290.

Moosavie, S. M. (1986). A sociolinguistic analysis of the Persian system of *taarof* and its implication for teaching of Farsi: University of Texas at Austin.

Mori, J. (2004). *Negotiating Agreement and Disagreement in Japanese: Connective expressions and turn construction.* Amsterdam/Philadelphia: John Benjamins.

Ochs, E. (1988). *Culture and Language Development. Language Acquisition and Language Socialization in a Samoan Village.* Cambridge: Cambridge University Press.

Ochs, E., Schegloff, E. A., & Thompson, S. A. (Eds.). (1996). *Interaction and Grammar.* Cambridge: Cambridge University Press.

Pasch, R. (1997). Weil mit Hauptsatz-Kuckucksei im denn-Nest [Weil 'because' in main clause-cucook's egg in denn 'since'-nest]. *Deutsche Sprache, 25*(3), 252–271.

Pomerantz, A. (1984). Agreeing and disagreeing with assessments: Some features of preferred/dispreferred turn shapes. In J. M. Atkinson & J. Heritage (Eds.), *Structures of Social Action* (pp. 225–246). Cambridge: Cambridge University Press.

Raymond, G. (2004). Prompting Action: the stand-alone "so" in ordinary conversation. *Research on Language and Social Interaction, 37*(2), 185–219.

Sacks, H. (1996). *Lectures on Conversation* (Vol. 1). ed. by Gail Jefferson, introduction by Emanuel Schegloff. Oxford: Blackwell.

Sacks, H., Schegloff, E. A., & Jefferson, G. (1974). A simplest systematics for the organization of turn-taking for conversation. *Language, 50*(4), 696–735.

Schegloff, E. A. (1968). Sequencing in conversational openings. *American Anthropologist, 70,* 1075–1095.

Schegloff, E. A. (1979). The relevance of repair to syntax-for-conversation. *Syntax and Semantics, 12*(Discourse and Syntax), 261–286.

Schegloff, E. A. (1980). Preliminaries to preliminaries: "Can I ask you a question?" *Sociological Inquiry, 50*(3–4), 104–151.

Schegloff, E. A. (1982). *Discourse as an interactional achievement: some uses of 'uh huh' and other things that come between sentences.* In D. Tannen (Ed.), *Analysing Discourse: Text and Talk* (pp. 71–93). Washington D.C.: Georgetown University Press.

Schegloff, E. A. (1984). On some questions and ambiguities in conversation. In J. M. Atkinson & J. Heritage (Eds.), *Structures of Social Action. Studies in Conversation Analysis* (pp. 28–52). Cambridge: Cambridge University Press.

Schegloff, E. A. (1988). Presequences and indirection. Applying speech act theory to ordinary conversation. *Journal of Pragmatics, 12*, 55–62.

Schegloff, E. A. (1990). On the organization of sequences as a source of "coherence" in talk-in-interaction. In B. Dorval (Ed.), *Conversational Organization and its Development* (pp. 51–77). Norwood, NJ: Ablex Publishing Corporation.

Schegloff, E. A. (in press). *A Primer in Conversation Analysis: Sequence Organization.* Cambrdige, England: Cambridge University Press.

Schegloff, E. A. (1996). Turn organization: One intersection of grammar and interaction. In E. Ochs, E. A. Schegloff & S. A. Thompson (Eds.), *Interaction and Grammar* (pp. 52–133). Cambridge: Cambridge University Press.

Schegloff, E. A., Ochs, E., & Thompson, S. A. (1996). Introduction. In E. Ochs, E. A. Schegloff & S. A. Thompson (Eds.), *Interaction and Grammar* (pp. 1–51). Cambridge: Cambridge University Press.

Schegloff, E. A., & Sacks, H. (1973). Opening up Closings. *Semiotica, 8*, 289–327.

Scheutz, H. (2001). On causal clause combining: The case of "weil" in spoken German. In M. Selting & E. Couper-Kuhlen (Eds.), *Studies in Interactional Linguistics* (pp. 111–141). Amsterdam/Philadelphia: John Benjamins.

Schlobinski, P. (1992). Nexus durch weil. In P. Schlobinski (Ed.), *Funktionale Grammatik und Sprachbeschreibung. Eine Untersuchung zum gesprochenen Deutsch sowie zum Chinesischen* [*Functional grammar and language description. A study of spoken German and Chinese*] (pp. 315–344). Opladen: Westdeutscher Verlag.

Scott, M. B., & Lyman, S. M. (1968). Accounts. *American Sociological Review, 33*, 46–62.

Scott, P. J. (1987). *The implications of a conversation analysis approach to request sequences for English language teaching.* Unpublished Thesis.

Scotton, C. M., & Bernstein, J. (1988). Natural conversations as a model for textbook dialogue. *Applied Linguistics, 9*(4), 372–384.

Seedhouse, P. (1998). CA and the analysis of foreign language interaction: A reply to Wagner. *Journal of Pragmatics, 30*, 85–102.

Selting, M. (1997). Sogenannte "Ellipsen" als interaktiv relevante Konstruktionen? Ein neuer Versuch über die Reichweite und Grenzen des Ellipsenbegriffs für die Analyse gesprochener Sprache in der konversationellen Interaktion [The so called "ellipsis" as interactional relevant construction? A new attempt about the expansion limits of the term ellipsis for the analysis of spoken language in conversational interaction]. In P. Schlobinski (Ed.), *Syntax des gesprochenen Deutsch* [*Syntax of spoken German*] (pp. 117–157). Opladen: Westdeutscher Verlag.

Selting, M., & Couper-Kuhlen, E. (Eds.). (2001). *Studies in interactional linguistics.* Amsterdam/Philadelphia: John Benjamins.

Sifianou, M. (1993). Off-record indirectness and the notion of imposition. *Multilingua, 12*(1), 69–79.

Sorjonen, M.-L. (1996). On repeats and responses in Finnish conversation. In E. Ochs, E. A. Schegloff & S. A. Thompson (Eds.), *Interaction and Grammar* (pp. 277–327). Cambrdige: Cambridge University Press.

Sorjonen, M.-L. (2001a). *Responding in Conversation: A study of response particles in Finnish.* Amsterdam/Philadelphia: John Benjamins.

Sorjonen, M.-L. (2001b). Simple answers to polar questions: The case of Finnish. In M. Selting & E. Couper-Kuhlen (Eds.), *Studies in Interactional Linguistics* (pp. 405–431). Amsterdam/ Philadelphia: John Benjamins.

Sorjonen, M.-L. (2002). Recipient activities: The particle *no* as a go-ahead response in Finnish conversations. In C. E. Ford, B. A. Fox & S. A. Thompson (Eds.), *The Language of Turn and Sequence* (pp. 165–195). Oxford: Oxford University Press.

Streeck, J. (1995). On projection. In E. N. Goody (Ed.), *Social intelligence and interaction: Expressions and implications of the social bias in human interaction* (pp. 87–111). Cambridge: Cambridge University Press.

Sweetser, E. (1990). *From etymology to pragmatics: Metaphorical and cultural aspects of semantic structure.* Cambridge: Cambridge University Press.

Taleghani-Nikazm, C. (1999). *Politeness in Native/Nonnative Speaker Interaction: Some manifestations of Persian Taarof in the Interaction among Iranian Speakers of German with German native speakers.* Unpublished Doctoral Dissertation, University of Texas, Austin.

Taleghani-Nikazm, C. (2005). Contingent requests: Their sequential organization and turn shape. *Research on Language and Social Interaction, 38*(2), 159–179.

Trosborg, A. (1995). *Interlanguage Pragmatics.* Berlin: Mouton de Gruyter.

Turk, M. J. (2004). Unisng *and* in Conversational Interaction. *Research on Language and Social Interaction, 37*(2), 219–250.

Uhmann, S. (1996). Nur ein Sturm im Lexikonglas. Zur aktuellen Verbstellungsvariation in weil-Sätzen [Only a storm in lexicon glass. On the recent variation of verb placement in weil 'because'-clauses]. *Wuppertaler Arbeiten zur Sprachwissenschaft, 13,* 1–26.

Uhmann, S. (1998). Verbstellungsvariation in weil-Sätzen: Lexikalische Differenzierung mit grammatischen Folgen [Variation of Verb Placement in weil-Clauses: Lexical Differentiation with Grammatical Consequences]. *Zeitschrift für Sprachwissenschaft, 17*(1), 92–139.

Uhmann, S. (2001). Some arguments for the relevance of syntax to same-sentence self-repair in everyday German conversation. In M. Selting & E. Couper-Kuhlen (Eds.), *Studies in Interactional Linguistics* (pp. 373–405). Amsterdam/Philadelphia: John Benjamins.

Van Mulken, M. (1996). Politeness markers in French and Dutch requests. *Language Sciences, 18*(3–4), 689–702.

Wahrig: Fehlerfreies und gutes Deutsch [Free of errors and good German]. (Vol. 5)(2003). Vol. 5). München: Wissen Media Verlag GmbH.

Wegener, H. (1993). *weil-das hat schon seinen Grund*: Zur Verbstellung in Kausalsätzen mit *weil* im gegenwärtigen Deutsch [*because-that has its reason*: About verb position in causal-clauses with *weil* in contemporary German]. *Deutsche Sprache, 4,* 289–306.

Wong, J. (2002). "Applying" Conversation Analysis in Applied Linguistics: Evaluating Dialogue in English as a Second Language Textbooks. *IRAL, 40*(1), 37–60.

Wooton, A. J. (1981). The management of grantings and rejections by parents in request sequences. *Semiotica, 37*(1/2), 59–89.

Appendix

The following abbreviations for grammatical descriptions are used in the inter-linear gloss:

AUX   auxiliary verb
MP   modal particle
RXP   reflexive pronoun
PR   preposition
PRX   prefix
SBJ   subjunctive

Name index

Subject index

In the series *Studies in Discourse and Grammar* the following titles have been published thus far or are scheduled for publication: